State and Islam in Baathist Syria

St Andrews Papers on Contemporary Syria

SERIES EDITOR, RAYMOND HINNEBUSCH

State and Islam in Baathist Syria

Confrontation or Co-optation?

Line Khatib, Raphaël Lefèvre, and Jawad Qureshi

University of St Andrews Centre for Syrian Studies

© 2012 by the University of St Andrews Centre for Syrian Studies

Published by the University of St Andrews Centre for Syrian Studies
School of International Relations
Fife, Scotland
UK

All rights reserved. No part of this publication may be reproduced or
transmitted in any form or by any means without prior permission of the publisher.

Distributed throughout the world by
Lynne Rienner Publishers, Inc.
1800 30th Street
Boulder, CO 80301
USA
www.rienner.com

British Library Cataloguing-in-Publication Data
A catalogue record for this book is available from the British Library.

Printed and bound in the United States of America

ISBN: 978-0-9568732-0-0

Contents

Foreword: State and Islam under Bashar al-Assad   1
    Raymond Hinnebusch

1   Hama and Beyond: Regime–Muslim Brotherhood   3
    Relations since 1982
    Raphaël Lefèvre

2   Islamic Revival and the Promotion of Moderate Islam   29
    from Above
    Line Khatib

3   The Discourses of the Damascene Sunni 'Ulama   59
    during the Revolution
    Jawad Qureshi

References   *93*
About the Authors   *99*

Foreword: State and Islam under Bashar al-Assad

Raymond Hinnebusch

The three papers in this issue of the St Andrews Papers provide a comprehensive overview of the relation between the Baathist state and Islam in Syria, with one picking up where the other leaves off. Each of the contributions is based on contemporary fieldwork and provides both new and unique empirical information and sophisticated analysis.

The first article by Raphaël Lefèvre is particularly valuable in providing an account of the perceptions of the Muslim Brotherhood (*Ikhwan*) leaders on the origins of the conflict in 1976-82, which culminated in the bloody showdown at Hama, as well as how they saw the subsequent negotiations conducted with the regime. His account benefits from interviews with many of the top Ikhwan leaders. In their view, repression by the Baath provoked the rise of radicals on the fringe of the organization who, in turn, forced a military confrontation with the regime that dragged in the whole Ikhwan organization. There are some parallels between this account and similar events in Egypt in the 1990s and perhaps Algeria. In addition, the Baath regime thereafter skillfully exploited divisions within the Ikhwan over responsibility for the Hama tragedy between the radical Hama and pragmatic Aleppo factions.

The contribution by Line Khatib highlights one consequence of the fraught relation between the regime and political Islam, namely the former's effort to foster and co-opt a non-political, often Sufi, Islam to counterbalance and undermine radical political Islam. Additionally, regime tolerance of this Islamic civil society was pursued as part of a divide and rule strategy of "authoritarian upgrading:" the regime could play off the Islamist and secular segments of society while posing as the main bulwark against the former in order to keep the later quiescent. As Khatib underlines, however, Islamist sheikhs were no mere pawns in this game and in some respects they were also using the state, even as it used them, to achieve the widening Islamization of society. They benefitted, in particular, from the regime's intolerance of any secular political discourse not under its control. This had at least partly unforeseen consequences and arguably facilitated an Islamization of society that helps explain the tangent of the 2011 Uprising.

The final contribution by Jawad Qureshi brings the narrative up to the 2011 Uprising, in which Sunni Islamic elements have played a major role. He provides examples of discourse by pivotal 'ulama from the beginnings of the protests, exposing the differences of opinions among them. What is notable is the evolution of their discourse from cautioning against *fitna* to defence of the right to protest, in parallel to the regime's use of violent repression against protestors. The Syrian 'ulama had to balance the costs of civil strife against the costs of remaining silent in the face of escalating repression and, in their ambivalent and changing stances, they likely reflect the opinions of wider society. Qureshi's survey underlines the possibility that, had the regime responded in a more restrained way to the protests, what started as demands for reform might not have escalated to the brink of civil war.

1
Hama and Beyond: Regime–Muslim Brotherhood Relations since 1982

Raphaël Lefèvre

Despite the long exile into which it has been forced since 1982, Syria's Muslim Brotherhood continues to be blamed for being behind the worst evils striking Syrian society. Bashar al-Assad even accused the exiled organization of having fomented the recent uprisings in his country since March 2011, described as a struggle pitting secular pan-Arabism against Islamism. In a comment reflecting the bitter relations entertained by the Syrian Ba'ath with the *Ikhwan* ("the Brotherhood"), the President added: "we've been fighting the Muslim Brotherhood since the 1950s and we are still fighting with them."[1]

Since Syrian independence from Mandatory France in 1946, the opposition between the two forces has to a large extent come to dominate the country's political scene. Within the framework of Syria's parliamentary democracy, the struggle between the Syrian Ba'ath and the Ikhwan remained at first largely peaceful. After the Ba'ath takeover of March 1963, however, and especially after Hafiz al-Assad's ascent to power in November 1970, the fight took on an increasingly violent dimension. Both forces became engaged in a bloody struggle, which would culminate in the massacre of thousands of Muslim Brothers by the regime in Hama in February 1982. While militarily defeated, the Islamic organization did not give up all political activities, continuing instead its opposition to the Syrian Ba'ath from abroad. In turn, the regime sought to exploit the divisions which have historically plagued the Muslim Brotherhood's ranks. It also frustrated the Islamic movement by at times opening up the door to allowing its return to Syria, at times closing down all possibility of a negotiated settlement between the two forces. Fraught with manipulations of all kinds and sporadic violence on both parts, the confrontation which has continued to pit the Syrian Ba'ath against the Muslim Brotherhood since the time of the Hama massacre deserves closer examination in order to understand the apparent bitterness which until today characterizes the relationship between Syria's two most significant political forces.

The tragedy of Hama: turning a peaceful opposition into a violent confrontation

If the relationship between the Ikhwan and the Ba'ath continues to be fraught with mutual mistrust despite the geographical distance setting them apart, it is largely due to the shared memory of the bloody spiral of violence which both forces were sucked into throughout much of the late 1970s and early 1980s, each side still blaming the other for the unprecedented high level of violence which the confrontation then assumed. A brief glance at the period surrounding the Hama massacre is therefore needed in order to understand the bitterness which has contaminated the relations between both forces ever since. The massacre of thousands of Muslim Brothers in the city of Hama, in February 1982, was the result of two self-reinforcing and antagonistic trends: the regime's more visible sectarian face assumed throughout the 1970s and the Ikhwan's subsequent radicalization.

Ideologically, the Ba'ath Party and the Ikhwan had always been at odds. The former was created in the mid-1940s by a Sunni Muslim, Salah Eddine al-Bitar, and a Christian Orthodox, Michel Aflaq, giving the party a cross-sectarian composition from the outset and also symbolizing the Party's attachment to the notion of a secularism that would embrace all religions within Arabism. With a slogan such as "religion is for God, country is for all",[2] the early Ba'athists were set to clash with Muslim Brothers convinced, for their part, that "Islam is both religion and state".[3] The first battle, within the framework of Syria's fledging parliamentary democracy, took place in February 1950 when members of the Ikhwan led by their historic founder, Mustapha al-Sibai, put forward a draft constitution containing a clause which, to the outrage of Ba'athist Members of Parliament, planned to make Islam the official "state religion" of the country. Eventually, the Ikhwan had to compromise and it was agreed that Islam would instead be the religion of the Head of State. Upon the Ba'ath Party's ascent to power in March 1963, however, the opposition between the two political forces assumed a more violent tone. As early as in April 1964, bloody clashes spread throughout Syria while concentrating heavily on the city of Hama. There, according to Syria's former Vice President and Governor of Hama at the time, Abdel Halim Khaddam, the angry crowd – initially protesting against the dismissal of two pious teachers who had vocally disagreed with the secular Ba'athist line – quickly turned into a violent anti-regime protest.[4] Led by Marwan Hadid, a radical Islamist militant, the demonstrations took on a bloody dimension when the insurgents gathered inside the Sultan Mosque, subsequently bombed by governmental troops. While not having been openly supported by the then-Ikhwani leader, Issam al-Attar, the memory of the 1964 Hama riots would nonetheless continue to haunt Islamic militants in the city, where a group of young radical activists would give rise, a few years later, to the emergence of a jihadist organization known as *al-Talia al-Muqatila* ("The Fighting Vanguard").

Already alienated by the secular Ba'athist line, the Brotherhood was also estranged from the economic programme carried out by the Ba'ath Party in power throughout the 1960s. The nationalizations and land reforms put forward by the Ba'athists, and especially the state takeover of foreign trade and some wholesale trade operations, were hurting the very constituency from which the Ikhwan was drawing its support, especially the urban traders. The antagonism between the two political forces heightened over the years as the regime became dominated by a new generation of Ba'athist activists whose radically different background gave rise to the so-called "neo-Ba'ath".[5] Strong within the military wing of the Ba'ath, originating from the countryside, from a modest background and, perhaps most significantly, often belonging to a religious minority, the new Ba'athists rulers led by Alawite General Salah Jadid carried out policies of a more radical outlook –including a militant secularism. It was, however, with the ascent to power of Hafiz al-Assad in November 1970 that the confrontation between the regime and the Ikhwan took an unprecedented turn. If at first relations between the two forces remained peaceful due to Hafiz al-Assad's more centrist position compared to his "neo-Ba'ath" predecessors, a single spark was bound to enflame the situation.

This came about in January 1973 when the Syrian leader published a draft constitution which, to the outrage of the religious sheikhs and the Muslim Brotherhood led by the young ideologue Said Hawwa, did not give Islam the special status it had been enjoying ever since the enactment of the 1950 constitution. Anti-regime demonstrations protesting against the "godless" Ba'ath erupted in many Syrian cities, concentrating once again in pious Hama. While the secular outlook of the Syrian Ba'ath was fiercely criticized by the protestors, there was also a growing feeling that the secularism advocated by the Ba'athist rulers was merely a pretext for the advancement of the interests of minority religious communities, especially the Alawites, who despite representing approximately 10% of the population concentrated in their hands Syria's most significant security and politico-economic institutions. Once a community marginalized from the centres of power by the Sunni majority – representing approximately 70% of the Syrian population – the Alawites had throughout the 1950s and 1960s risen to such prominence inside the armed forces and the Ba'ath that some started to refer to an "Alawite plot" destined to take over Syria. At any rate, Hafiz al-Assad had become the first President of Syria from an Alawite background, giving apparent credit to the thesis that his regime was a sectarian one.

The seemingly more sectarian face assumed by the regime, a feature which appeared to many as increasingly visible in the light of Hafiz al-Assad's June 1976 intervention against the Palestine Liberation Organization (PLO) in Lebanon, progressively radicalized a wide margin of Syria's Sunni Muslim population, who found in the Muslim Brotherhood and its more radical offshoots a convenient vehicle to express their resentment against the Assad regime. In turn, the Muslim Brotherhood itself radicalized its tactics and ideology throughout the 1970s. Once a conservative organization led by pragmatic leaders committed to a peaceful approach to politics, like Mustapha al-Sibai and Issam al-Attar, it had become in the 1970s dominated by a group of young activists whose radical outlook gave a more overtly sectarian tone to the Ikhwan's discourse. Islamic publications affiliated with the Muslim Brotherhood, such as *al-Nadhir*, increasingly referred to the "Alawite enemy" and to those "infidel Nusayri [i.e. Alawites] who are outside of Islam".[6] Said Hawwa, a radical Islamic thinker from Hama who had become, by 1975, the Muslim Brotherhood's main ideologue, referred back to Ibn Taymiyya's controversial fatwa condemning the Alawites in a bid to draw support for the Ikhwan.

The organization's newfound radicalism represented a critical departure from the more moderate, earlier Ikhwani line. The "Damascus wing" – a group of moderate Muslim Brothers, mostly stemming from the Syrian capital, who had rallied around Issam al-Attar's leadership throughout the 1960s – had by the early 1970s broken away from the organization. At the time, the split did not have an ideological dimension. Rather than reflecting the division of the organization between "radicals" and "moderates", the split concerned the resentment expressed by a "Northern axis" comprising Ikhwani members from Aleppo, Hama and Latakia against the disproportionate regional representation of Damascus inside the leadership of the organization.[7] The then-Ikhwani leader, Issam al-Attar, was also criticized by many Muslim Brothers for lacking leadership skills –confusing "being a great speaker with being a great leader",[8] analysts suggested. In addition, others explained that his exile to Europe after 1964 had made communication with the rest of the organization in Syria more difficult. When, in 1969, Issam al-Attar's leadership of the movement was successfully challenged by prominent members of the "Northern Axis", he and his Damascene followers resigned in protest.

At any rate, the departure of the more moderate Ikhwani members of the Muslim Brotherhood from the early 1970s onwards certainly contributed to fostering an ideological and political void, into which younger and more radical activists stepped. During the first half of the 1970s, the organization was led by Sheikh Abdel Fatah Abu Ghuddah, a respected Islamic scholar from Aleppo, who had little political ambitions. The radical turn came about in 1975 when Abu Ghuddah handed over the leadership of the Ikhwan to the more hard-line Adnan Saadeddine from Hama, a controversial figure blamed by many until today for having plunged the organization into a violent confrontation with the regime. While not openly calling for "jihad" against the Syrian Ba'ath until 1980, Adnan Saadeddine's troops nonetheless started to prepare for an armed resistance against the regime.

In that endeavour, they were deeply influenced by the growing popularity of the above-mentioned al-Talia al-Muqatila –a jihadist organization which had emerged on the fringes of the Ikhwan. In line with the "Qutbist"[9] thought gaining ground at the time, al-Talia's legendary leader, Marwan Hadid, was ambitious to pose as the "Vanguard" of the Muslim Brotherhood by directly targeting the regime's symbols –by the same token drawing the Ikhwan into an immediate confrontation with the Syrian Ba'ath. The jihadist organization, at first heavily present in Hama, widened its geographical base upon Marwan Hadid's death by torture in 1976, after his successor, Abdel Sattar az-Zaim, organized a more co-ordinated network of cells throughout Syria destined to take revenge for their leader's assassination. It is worth stressing that the extent to which the Muslim Brotherhood and al-Talia al-Muqatila co-ordinated their actions between 1977 and 1980 is still open to debate –the regime insisting they formed a single organization while the Ikhwan claims it had nothing to do with the jihadist group. However, while Ikhwani leaders are keen to stress that the Muslim Brotherhood expelled from the organization any members known to also belong to al-Talia, others suggest that, in Hama at least, membership became blurred.

Adnan Saadeddine, the Hama-born leader of the Ikhwan at the time, seems to have been particularly active in attempting to strengthen the informal ties between the two organizations. According to Ali Sadreddine al-Bayanouni, an Aleppo-born prominent member of the

Ikhwan, who would rise to the leadership of the movement in the late 1990s, Adnan Saadeddine had undertaken to bring al-Talia under the Brotherhood's wing despite the Ikhwan's collective decision to not join forces with the jihadist organization. "There was a meeting between Adnan Saadeddine and Abdel Satar az-Zaim at Beyrouth in January 1977. But this was not an official encounter, it was a discussion between two individuals and did not involve the Muslim Brotherhood's leadership",[10] he stresses. Zouheir Salem, an Ikhwani member from Aleppo and now spokesman for the organization, goes as far as claiming that, at the time, Adnan Saadeddine started smuggling arms from Iraq without even consulting the movement's leadership.[11] Allegations that in Hama, al-Talia and the Ikhwan had merged under the impulse of Hamawites Adnan Saadeddine and his ideologue Said Hawwa are, for their part, fiercely denied by Muhammed Riyadh al-Shuqfah, then leader of the local branch of the Muslim Brotherhood. While he remembers that in Hama there were indeed "personal friendships" between the local leaders of the Ikhwan and members of al-Talia, he stresses that there was never a real coordination of actions between the two organizations before 1980 but merely "cash transfers from the Brotherhood to al-Talia destined to help the families of those injured, killed or arrested by the Ba'athist authorities".[12]

At any rate, al-Talia was successful in its ambition to act as the vanguard of the Islamic movement insofar as its violent activism ultimately triggered a governmental retaliation so fierce that it dragged the entire Muslim Brotherhood into an overt struggle with the Ba'athist regime. Already subject to fierce repression throughout the 1970s, members of the Ikhwan had to go entirely underground after al-Talia leader Adnan Uqlah organized the slaughter of 82 Alawite Cadets at the Aleppo Artillery School in June 1979. While this sectarian massacre was quickly condemned by Adnan Saadeddine and the whole leadership of the Muslim Brotherhood, the Ba'athist regime insisted on blaming the massacre on the Ikhwan, refusing to draw a distinction between al-Talia and the Brotherhood and heightening its repression against the Islamic movement. "The situation became untenable", says Zouheir Salem, who was in Aleppo at the time. "The leadership of the movement was shocked: we did not know who the perpetrators of the [Aleppo Artillery School] attack were, a crisis was unfolding and we could feel it", he remembers. Walid Safour, a London-based human rights activist who was then living in Homs, recalls that the June 1979 attack marked a turning point in the intensity of the repression suffered by those accused of belonging to the Muslim Brotherhood. "From then-on, life became a hell: I was arrested several times between June 1979 and October 1980 and tortured so severely by the Military Intelligence that I would later need to undergo three surgeries, leaving my back disabled until today".[13] Then, in retaliation against an attempt aiming at Hafiz al-Assad's life, two units of Rifaat al-Assad's Defence Companies were sent to Palmyra, where Ba'athist officers slaughtered at least 500 suspected members of the Ikhwan, jailed in a prison located in the surrounding desert. On 8th July, the Syrian Parliament passed the notorious "Law No. 49", which until today makes it a capital offense to belong to the Muslim Brotherhood.

"We had no other option but to defend ourselves", argues today Ali Sadreddine al-Bayanouni, who became one of the first "military commanders" of the Ikhwan when the organization set up an armed branch in October 1979. Under the leadership of Hassan al-Houeidi, a prominent Ikhwan from Deir ez-Zoor, the Muslim Brotherhood formed a "Joint Command" tasked with co-ordinating Ikhwani actions with those of Adnan Uqlah's al-Talia al-Muqatila as well as Issam al-Attar's "Damascus wing". Accounts differ on the extent to which the "Joint Command" carried out violent activities against the regime. Muhammed Hawari, a long-time member of the "Damascus wing", claims that Issam al-Attar's faction made its adherence to the "Joint Command" dependent upon al-Talia and the Ikhwan accepting to refrain from the use of arms against the regime.[14] It is certain, however, that Adnan Uqlah's al-Talia al-Muqatila did not cease its violent activities. In addition, the Brotherhood for its part maintains that it kept carrying out "defensive actions" throughout the early 1980s. "Things became blurred as an increasing number of Ikhwani activists also started to individually join al-Talia",[15] adds Zouheir Salem who, in addition, suggests that this was particularly the case in the city of Hama. When this bastion of religious orthodoxy became the focal point of the anti-regime movement throughout 1981 and early 1982, a profound rift started to emerge between Ikhwani members originating from Hama and those from Aleppo.

"Hamawite members of the Muslim Brotherhood perceived the situation differently than [Aleppine Ikhwanis] did, they had a different thinking", explains Ali Saddredine al-Bayanouni in a recent interview. While those originating from the conservative city expressed an eagerness to do whatever it would take to defend their hometown from Ba'athist tanks, those from Aleppo seemed more cautious not to provoke the regime into a last-ditch battle before the Ikhwan was certain it had chances of winning it. Ultimately, however, the former won the advantage over the latter. Said Hawwa, a young radical ideologue who also acted as Adnan Saadeddine's right hand man, reportedly threatened

Ali Saddredine al-Bayanouni that, if he did not pass on his job as "military commander" of the Brotherhood, Hawwa would resign from the organization. While still open to debate, the role played by Said Hawwa in the subsequent unfolding of events seems to have been crucial. Having taken over as head of the "military branch" of the Ikhwan in January 1982, a few weeks before the violent Hama uprisings, he appears to have pushed the Brotherhood into an overt confrontation with the regime.

After Adnan Uqlah left his Jordanian exile in January 1982 for Hama, where he warned the city's inhabitants that he would soon send them a codeword signalling that the time had come to rise against the regime's presence, the zealous leader of al-Talia was immediately summoned back to Amman by the Brotherhood's leadership, who disagreed with him on the immediacy of "jihad". According to the Ikhwan's Hama branch leader Muhammed Riyadh al-Shuqfah, who was present in Amman when the events occurred, the Ikhwan's Executive Committee, then headed by Hassan al-Houeidi, asked Said Hawwa to send a letter to the local leader of al-Talia in Hama, Umar Jawad, instructing him to not follow Adnan Uqlah's orders. The message, however, never reached Umar Jawad. When Adnan Uqlah broadcast, from a radio station based in neighbouring Iraq, the codeword for "jihad" against the Ba'ath in Hama, the local troops of al-Talia and of the Ikhwan rose as a single man, distributing weapons to the city's inhabitants and provoking the violent uprisings which would trigger a disproportionate governmental response causing between 20,000 and 40,000 deaths.[16] There is still considerable controversy inside the movement as to how the message destined to Umar Jawad became "lost" between Amman and Hama, underlining the still-existing mistrust and, to a certain extent, tension pitting Ikhwanis from Hama against those from Aleppo. Muhammed Riyadh al-Shuqfah, a long-time member of the "Hama clan", thus asserts that his colleague Said Hawwa did send the message to Umar Jawad and that the messenger, a trusted driver, should therefore be blamed for having "lost" it.[17] Others belonging to the "Aleppo faction", such as Zouheir Salem, suggest that, given Said Hawwa's particularly hard-line stance against the Ba'ath, he might not have wished to follow the Executive Committee's orders and instead went his own way, tacitly supporting Adnan Uqlah's jihadist effort.[18] When asked why Said Hawwa subsequently resigned from the Brotherhood's Executive Committee in 1983, Ali Saddredine al-Bayanouni explains that the radical Ikhwani ideologue might have felt a "special responsibility"[19] for the tragic way the Hama uprisings ended.

Beyond its unprecedented human cost, the tragedy of Hama also ushered a period of unparalleled political paralysis in Syrian politics. The Muslim Brotherhood, the most significant opposition force to the Ba'ath before the Hama massacre, had been militarily defeated. By terribly increasing the repression against the once-peaceful Islamic movement, the Syrian Ba'ath had managed to turn the organization into a violent one, ripped by internal divisions over how to best deal with a ruthless regime. The regime's tactic – which is not without current parallels – proved successful insofar as the period following the Hama massacre became turbulent for the deeply divided Islamic movement.

After Hama: exploiting the Muslim Brotherhood's divisions

For many inside the Muslim Brotherhood, Hama had been a trap too easily set up by a Ba'athist regime keen to suck the Muslim Brotherhood's most radical elements into a fatal last-ditch battle. According to Muhammed Riyadh al-Shuqfah, what began as a political struggle between the leadership of the Muslim Brotherhood and the Syrian Ba'ath eventually took the form of a military fight between the most hardline Ba'athist figure, Rif'at al-Assad, and the zealous "Caliph", Adnan Uqlah.[20] Provoked by the regime, the battle of Hama opened deep wounds of mistrust among Ikhwanis over who in the movement was to be blamed for the tragic unfolding of events. "Hama was like an earthquake for the Muslim Brotherhood. The differences among us surfaced and some of us started looking for scapegoats",[21] recounted Adnan Saadeddine. For many Hamawites, it was Adnan Uqlah's troops who were responsible for the violence which seized Hama in early February 1982 –even though the distinction between many of Uqlah's men and Ikhwani Hamawites was not always clear cut. At any rate, Adnan Uqlah quickly became a convenient scapegoat for Ikhwani Hamawites. Shortly after the Hama events, Adnan Saadeddine thus declared that "all of Adnan Uqlah's actions proceeded from want of prudence, undue haste or sheer recklessness", stressing that the leader of al-Talia had brought "considerable damage" to the Islamic movement due to the way he "conducted the fighting in Aleppo" and "drew the mujahidin into the ill-timed confrontation at Hama".[22] However, the sense of lasting bitterness still found among Ikhwani ranks at the evocation of the 1982 events has less opposed members of the Muslim Brotherhood to the activists of al-Talia than pitted Ikhwanis from Aleppo against those from Hama. Eventually, the former indeed accused the latter of having been the real driving force behind the movement's radicalization at the time.

The blame game was eventually settled as the Muslim Brotherhood's consultative body, the Majlis al-Shura, decided from its Jordanian exile to set up a special committee headed by Syrian Brother Muhammed Ali Ashmi and tasked with investigating what had gone wrong inside the movement. Perhaps unsurprisingly, Adnan Saadeddine and Said Hawwa were very reluctant at the idea of having a "truth-seeking committee" being set up, remembers Muhammed Riyadh al-Shuqfah.[23] Due to their fierce opposition, the evaluation report was never made publicly available and its content remains, to this very day, a closely guarded secret. According the researcher Alison Pargeter, it reportedly lay much of the blame on the person of Adnan Saadeddine, accused of having set up, in 1977, a special committee tasked with secretly coordinating actions with al-Talia al-Muqatila –something which the former Ikhwani leader has denied in a booklet defending his legacy.[24] At any rate, the accusation exacerbated the already existing tensions between the "Aleppo faction" and the "Hama clan". The first group, principally based in Amman, had by the mid-1980s regrouped around Sheikh Abdel Fattah Abu Ghuddah while the other, led by Adnan Saadeddine, had settled in neighbouring Iraq.

Ikhwani members from Hama were still bitter at the destruction of their hometown by the Ba'athist troops and continued to advocate armed struggle against the regime. In its endeavour, the "Hama clan" could benefit from material and financial assistance from the competing Ba'athist regime in Baghdad. According to al-Shuqfah, who was in the Iraqi capital on the side of Adnan Saadeddine at the time, the "Hama clan" had high-level contacts at the top echelons of the regime headed by Saddam Hussein. The Iraqi leader had reportedly put Taha Yassin al-Ramadan, his Vice-President, in charge of the relations with the Syrian Brotherhood.[25] The Iraqi regime, embroiled in an irreconcilable dispute with Damascus since the 1970s, provided the Syrian Islamic movement with arms, money and training camps used by the young members of the Ikhwan who had regrouped in Baghdad following the Hama massacre. Thanks to this unexpected help, members of the Ikhwan affiliated with the "Hama clan" were able to carry out a few additional attacks inside Syria, prepared by a "military branch" headed by Farouk Tayfour.

"The Syrian regime knew very well that the Iraqi intelligence was providing support to the Ikhwan",[26] asserts the former Ba'athist Vice President of Syria, Abdel Halim Khaddam. In order to deter any members of the Ikhwan from becoming affiliated with a group or with an individual carrying out violent activities against the Syrian regime, the Ba'athist authorities undertook an intimidation campaign against prominent Muslim Brothers. Issam al-Attar recalls that, on 17th March

1981, a team of three men entered his house and slaughtered his wife, in an act surely destined to punish the leader of the "Damascus wing", who had just joined forces with al-Talia and the rest of the Brotherhood. Throughout the 1980s, his presence in Aachen continued to be considered such a serious threat to the security of the surrounding residents that the German government banned him from speaking in public and ordered him to change residence on a regular basis, in neighbourhoods as remote as possible from important residential areas.[27] Muhammed Riyadh al-Shuqfah, for his part, remembers having suffered from four assassination attempts while being in Baghdad, three of them being foiled by the Iraqi intelligence – thereby also underlining the extent to which Saddam Hussein's security apparatus was active in protecting Syrian Ikhwanis living on its territory.[28] It is also widely purported that Adnan Uqlah, the "Caliph" of al-Talia, was trapped and killed by the Syrian intelligence alongside the Syrian-Iraqi border sometime in late 1982.

The regime was quick to understand, however, that it could most effectively benefit from the internal divisions the Ikhwan suffered by stimulating the controversy over how the Brotherhood should best deal with the regime. In December 1984, Ali Duba, Hafiz al-Assad's head of Military Intelligence, contacted the then-leader of the Ikhwan, Hassan al-Houedi, to enquire as to whether the organization would be interested in carrying out negotiations potentially leading to a settlement of the dispute. While the Hamawite members of the Ikhwan were deeply reluctant to participate, they were nonetheless convinced by the rest of the organization that a dialogue with the regime, at such a catastrophic stage for the Islamic movement, was the only way forward. Several thousand members belonging to the Muslim Brotherhood had been forced to flee the repression they suffered in Syria, many of them finding refuge in Jordan, Iraq and, to a lesser extent, Saudi Arabia and Turkey. "Our situation was desperate", remembers Walid Safour, who fled to Jordan in 1979 before settling in London. "The organization did whatever it could to support us, providing a monthly assistance of around 30 Dinars to each refugee, but this was hardly enough in a country where 5 Dinars a day are needed to survive".[29]

Keen to seize every possible opportunity to have its members safely return to Syria, the Muslim Brotherhood accepted to meet Ali Duba to start negotiations with the Ba'athist regime. These took place in December 1984 in a hotel in Bonn, Germany, where Ali Duba and two of his aides, Nisham Bukhtiar and Hassan Khalil, met with the Syrian Ikhwan's leader, Hassan al-Houedi, assisted by Munir al-Ghadban and Muhammed Riyadh al-Shuqfah. According to the latter, who recalls the meeting, it quickly became clear that the regime's real aim was to provoke divisions within the Muslim Brotherhood by sowing confusion amongst its ranks. Thus, while Ali Duba and Hassan al-Houeidi isolated themselves in a separate room, suggesting progress was made towards a negotiated settlement, Hassan Khalil reportedly came to Muhammed Riyadh al-Shuqfah and expressed, for his part, a clear lack of willingness to proceed to the negotiations. Confused and exhausted after a day of talks and counter-talks, hope and disappointment, both camps agreed to take some rest before carrying on with the next round of negotiations. "A few hours later, Ali Duba telephoned Hassan al-Houeidi to report that the Syrian intelligence officers were on a train back to Berlin before taking off for Damascus; they had fooled us",[30] recalls with bitterness al-Shuqfah.

By proposing negotiations to the Ikhwan, the regime had achieved two goals: it had managed to re-open the painful internal debate over how the Ikhwan should best approach the Syrian Ba'ath and it had had a glimpse into how fractured and bitter the Muslim Brothers were in exile. "There never was any serious intent on the part of the regime to actually settle the dispute with the Muslim Brotherhood, these negotiations were doomed in advance", admits Abdel Halim Khaddam, the former Vice President of Syria. "The delegation led by Ali Duba suggested to the Ikhwan that they could be allowed to return to Syria but only under the condition that they do so as individuals and refrain from any political activity. In reality, the regime did not wish to see any form of agreement being reached with the Muslim Brotherhood",[31] he concludes.

If the regime's real intention was to sow division among Ikhwani ranks, it was successful. The frictions which opposed the "Hama clan" to the "Aleppo faction", already existing in 1982 and 1983, came to a head with the failure of the 1984 negotiations. Back in Baghdad, the Hamawites led by Adnan Saadeddine and Farouk Tayfour continued to plan attacks against Ba'athist installations inside Syria. The Aleppines, for their part, persisted in believing that negotiations with the regime were still the only way forward despite the failure of the earlier attempt. It was amidst this tactical dispute pitting those favourable to armed struggle against those privileging negotiations, that there emerged the 1986 leadership crisis in the organization. It opposed the moderate scholar Sheikh Abdel Fatah Abu Ghuddah, favourable to the pursuit of talks with the regime, to the more hard-line Adnan Saadeddine, for whom "there is nothing to discuss with these criminals; they are not a government, they are a mafia".[32] In retrospect, however, many Syrian Brothers recognized that the struggle for leadership between the Hamawite and Aleppine figures also had a strong personal dimension.

"The debate on armed struggle was a façade insofar as it provided a useful pretext to decide who should be the next leader and, in my opinion, Adnan Saadeddine was by far the best",[33] explains today al-Shuqfah. If from a different camp, Zouheir Salem agrees that ideology takes second place to a clash of personalities when it comes to explaining the roots behind the 1986 leadership struggle. "While Abu Ghuddah was a respected scholar with a broad outlook, Saadeddine had a narrow view of the situation and was an impulsive and individualistic character",[34] he asserts. To a certain extent, the leadership crisis opposing Saadeddine to Abu Ghuddah might also reflected cultural differences setting the members from Hama apart from those of Aleppo –the first being described as "men of action" while the second are often referred to as "the politicians". Between 1984 and 1985, elections opposing the two figures were held inside the movement and, since Abu Ghuddah's declared victory was not recognized by Saadeddine, an interim leadership was organized, putting Adeeb Jajeh and then Munir al-Ghdaban at the helm of the organization for six consecutive months each. Ultimately, however, Adnan Saadeddine unilaterally declared that he was taking up the leadership position, creating a rift of mistrust still felt to this day in relationships between Ikhwani members from Aleppo and those from Hama, who then largely rallied behind their chief.

By 1986, the personal, ideological and cultural differences setting the "Aleppo faction" apart from the "Hama clan" had effectively fractured the Islamic movement into two clearly distinct organizations. The first, led by Sheikh Abu Ghuddah, was recognized by the international body of the Muslim Brotherhood as the legitimate representative of the Syrian Ikhwan. It also adopted a more conciliatory stance towards the Ba'athist regime. A new round of negotiations between this organization and Ali Duba was carried out in Frankfurt throughout September 1987 –with no more success than the preceding talks. It has been reported that, when Hassan al-Houeidi met Ali Duba for the second time and asked that the security services release the thousands of Muslim Brothers still imprisoned inside Syria as a gesture of goodwill, Hafiz al-Assad's chief of military intelligence replied with arrogance: "But, you want the end of the regime!"[35] The Syrian Ba'ath, aware of the existing divisions separating the two wings of the Ikhwan, certainly intended to use the 1987 negotiations as a way to further exacerbate tensions within the Islamic movement. In retrospect, those inside the "Aleppo faction" who were responsible for the 1987 negotiations acknowledge they were aware of the risk that the regime might instrumentalize the talks to the detriment of the Ikhwan. "We knew that the regime wanted to play a game with us but we still thought that we should take up every opportunity to negotiate and give it a try, believing that by reaching out we would all move forward and that, in the end, progress would be made in the interest of all",[36] explained Ali Sadreddine al-Bayanouni in a recent interview.

By tantalizing the Muslim Brotherhood's moderates with the prospect of a settlement, Hafiz al-Assad was successful in exploiting the Islamic movement's inherent ideological contradictions. From Baghdad, Adnan Saadeddine's dissident Ikhwani organization fiercely criticized the "Aleppo faction" for having been lured again into the regime's negotiations trap. His "Hama clan" continued to be financially and materially supported by an Iraqi Ba'ath regime keen, for its part, to benefit from Adnan Saadeddine's presence in Baghdad to present itself with Islamic credentials. "For once in our lives, we were prized by the Ba'athists!",[37] remembers with irony Muhammed Riyadh al-Shuqfah. In turn, the "Hama clan" strove to support Saddam Hussein in the battles he fought on the regional and international arenas. While, throughout the 1980s, Adnan Saadeddine repeatedly blamed the "evil" Iranian regime for its war with Iraq; he also became, in the early 1990s, Saddam Hussein's personal envoy to the Islamic world. Obeida Nahas, a member of the "Aleppo faction", explains how close Adnan Saadeddine was to the regime in Baghdad: "When Iraq became targeted by UN sanctions following its invasion of Kuwait, he mounted public relations activities to persuade Islamic countries, especially across South East Asia, to support an isolated Saddam Hussein". For Obeida Nahas, Adnan Saadeddine's role in that respect became so prominent that, in his view, "it exceeded the role of Iraqi Embassies"[38] in this corner of the world. At any rate, the Iraqi regime's crucial support to the "Hama clan" allowed it to continue its armed campaign against the Syrian Ba'ath after the 1986 scission. Attacks claimed by Adnan Saadeddine's "Syrian Liberation Army" even touched the heart of the capital when bombs went off at Damascus' central bus station, killings hundreds of civilians on April 16th 1986.[39]

By 1990, the leadership of the officially-recognized branch of the Syrian Ikhwan had switched back again from Sheikh Abu Ghuddah, who at 70 years old had no more political ambitions, to Hassan al-Houeidi. Under the new leadership, efforts were made at reconciling the "Aleppo faction" with the "Hama clan". Eventually, much of the "Hama clan" accepted to progressively rejoin the main organization throughout 1991 and 1992, aware that armed action against the regime had not led anywhere and that the alliance with Iraq had somewhat constrained its autonomy. However, their historic leader, Adnan Saadeddine, was not allowed back into the wider organization. His membership in the movement had been "suspended" by the internationally-recognized faction after he had proclaimed himself leader of the movement in 1986 and it was not reinstated until 2008, shortly before he died in 2010. According to Zouheir Salem, a prominent member of the "Aleppo faction", much of the "Hama clan" accepted to rejoin the main organization in the early 1990s because they realized that the tensions which existed inside the movement did not pit Hama against Aleppo but, in reality, opposed the antagonistic personality of Adnan Saadeddine to the rest of the Ikhwan. "They eventually came to the realization that the problem came from within Hama",[40] he concludes.

Revolving doors: between conciliation and opposition from abroad

Since the early 1990s, the history of the Ikhwan has essentially been marked by the moderate ideological footprint left upon it by the "Aleppo faction", which had posed as a precondition for the 1991-1992 regrouping that the "Hama clan" renounces the use of violence against the regime. In that regard, the personal evolution underwent by the Ikhwan's leader throughout the late 1990s and 2000s, Ali Sadreddine al-Bayanouni from Aleppo, is revealing of the movement's progressive doctrinal moderation. Once a radical member of the "Aleppo faction" and one of the first "military commander" of the Muslim Brotherhood, he had by the early 2000s made his newfound commitment to non-violence, the protection of minorities and the promotion of democracy the cornerstone of Ikhwani discourse in exile.

As leader of the organization (1996-2010), his first steps were to soften the image of an organization tainted by its links to the violence of the early 1980s. In 2001, he pushed Ikhwani members to adopt a National Honour Charter which condemned in unequivocal terms the use of violence against one's own government. This effort culminated in the publication of the Muslim Brotherhood's political project in 2004, which represented a partial attempt at acknowledging part of the Ikhwan's responsibility for the bloody events of the late 1970s and early 1980s. The document stressed that, in the light of these events, "the Muslim Brotherhood in Syria has carried out a thorough review of its policies". It also acknowledged that "we, together with large numbers of Syrian citizens, found ourselves forced to resort to self-defence in a situation of spiralling violence that was certainly not of our making".[41] According to Zouheir Salem, often considered as the chief ideologue of today's Syrian Ikhwan, "the organization learned from the failure of armed struggle: we now believe that the only way forward is to oppose the regime through peaceful means on the model of Mustapha al-Sibai and Issam al-Attar".[42] Perhaps unsurprisingly, such doctrinal evolution was fiercely criticized by Adnan Saadeddine who, from Baghdad, reportedly went as far as pledging that he would rather chop off his own hand rather than agree to sign any official Ikhwani document stating a renouncement to armed action against the Syrian Ba'ath.[43] The former leader of the "Hama clan" seems to have been rather isolated in his struggle, however, as a growing number of Muslim Brothers started to voice hopes that their rejection of violence would allow them to negotiate more effectively a way back home.

If in the early 1980s the regime's attitude towards the Islamic movement had not been characterized by a particular willingness to compromise, things seemed to be changing in a positive direction throughout the rest of the 1980s and 1990s. A cable from the American Embassy in Damascus dated from February 1985 reported that a few hundred members from al-Talia al-Muqatila had returned to Syria after the regime carried out a negotiation with them through the mediation of Sa'id Shaban, a prominent Sunni Lebanese activist.[44] Throughout the 1990s, Hafiz al-Assad also proceeded to liberate prisoners who had been accused of belonging to the banned organization, most of them confined to jail since the late 1970s. Out of 10,000 estimated political prisoners, the Syrian President released 2,864 inmates in December 1991, 600 in March 1992, 554 in November 1993, 1,200 in November 1995, 250 in 1998 and 600 in November 2000.[45] Relations also seemed to be markedly improving between the Syrian Ikhwan's leadership and the Ba'athist regime. In December 1995, the Syrian authorities had allowed former Ikhwani leader Sheikh Abdel Fatah Abu Ghuddah to return to Aleppo, his city of birth, under the condition that he would occupy himself only with religious and educational work while giving up all political activities. Two years later, in February 1997, upon learning that Abu Ghuddah had just passed away, Hafiz al-Assad himself sent his condolences to the Islamic scholar's family, praising "a man who inspired respect during his lifetime",[46] in return earning the gratitude of the bereaved family. In this context, new mediation efforts between the Syrian Ba'ath and the Muslim Brotherhood's leadership were initiated. They were carried out through the intermediary of Amin Yagan, a former prominent Ikhwan who had distanced himself from the organization at the height of the violent confrontation. However, the negotiations soon proved fruitless as they came to reflect the regime's continued intention to accentuate divisions within the Islamic movement, according to Muhammed Riyadh al-Shuqfah. When Amin Yagan was assassinated in ambiguous circumstances on December 16th,

1998, the Ikhwan was quick to suspect the Ba'athist regime of having slain him and relations between the two parties deteriorated again.[47]

Upon Hafiz al-Assad's death in June 2000, brief hope was raised again that a leadership change at the top of the Syrian state apparatus would bring about a policy shift with regards to the fate of exiled Muslim Brotherhood members. From London, the leader of the organization, Ali Sadreddine al-Bayanouni, suggested that Bashar al-Assad's ascent to power could mean time had come for the Islamic movement to finally settle accounts with the Ba'athist regime. "Bashar has come into the weighty inheritance of decades of totalitarian rule; he does not bear responsibility for what happened in the past at Hama and in other places but only for what happens after he is sworn in [to office]",[48] he declared. Early signs seemed to indicate a certain willingness on the part of the regime to write a new chapter in its relation with the Islamic organization. According to the researcher Eyal Zisser, when in April 2001 the young President promulgated a decree ordering the issuance of one-year passports destined to encourage Syrian citizens abroad to return home to settle their affairs with the authorities, many interpreted this as a gesture indicating to Muslim Brotherhood members that they would be allowed to return to Syria as individuals. If a few of them did so, most of them nonetheless refrained from believing in the regime's promises. They had heard stories of a handful of Muslim Brothers returning home only to be interrogated, harassed, tortured and, in certain cases, killed by security services who asked them to fully confess their participation in the bloody events of the early 1980s. When, after a brief period of liberalization known as the "Damascus Spring", it became clear that Bashar al-Assad had no serious intention of reforming the political system he had inherited from his father, the Ikhwan started to call again for an overthrow of the Ba'athist regime. Having rejected violence, they started to engage in coalitions in exile with political forces distinct from theirs as a means to increase pressure on the Syrian Ba'ath from abroad, in line with the moderate spirit of their 2004 political project.

Such willingness to engage in a political dialogue with other Syrian opposition forces, be they ideologically antagonist to them, was not new to the Ikhwan. A few months after the Hama massacre, in April 1982, Muslim Brotherhood leaders had joined Salah Jedid's dissident Ba'athist faction as well as the Arab Socialist troops of Akram al-Hawrani in a National Alliance for the Liberation of Syria (NALS). The effort was short-lived, however, as the Iraqi location of the Alliance's headquarters and the bitter infighting resulting in Akram al-Hawrani's departure from it a few years later raised doubts over its sustainability as a credible opposition in exile. In the early 2000s, the Ikhwan expressed a renewed eagerness to join the dialogue carried out in the framework of the "Damascus Spring" by other Syrian opposition forces, including various prominent secular left-wing figures such as the Christian Michel Kilo and the Communist Riad al-Turk. Negotiations over a common opposition platform most notably culminated in October 2005 with the signing of the "Damascus Declaration", of which the Muslim Brotherhood became a key component.[49]

However, it was the defection of Abdel Halim Khaddam from Damascus in December 2005 which provided a real opportunity for the Syrian Ikhwan to prove that it was once again a pragmatic movement willing to go as far as engaging with former Ba'athist officials. According to the former Vice President, it was the Brotherhood which initiated the dialogue after Ali Sadreddine al-Bayanouni and Abdel Halim Khaddam had both taken part in a show broadcasted on *Al-Jazeera* in January 2006.[50] The two parties agreed to form a joint opposition platform which culminated with the creation of the National Salvation Front (NSF) at a meeting in Brussels in March 2006. For the Brotherhood, the alliance with the former Ba'athist Vice President represented a golden opportunity to regain a measure of relevance in the landscape of Syrian politics. According to Obeida Nahas, who was Bayanouni's political adviser, "this was a serious enterprise as we thought our partnership with a former prominent Ba'athist would attract more defections on the part of regime officials".[51] At the time, the belief that the NSF was gaining momentum was also shared by many inside the Ba'athist regime who expressed "fear"[52] at the emergence of such an alliance precisely when Bashar al-Assad's grip on power was being greatly weakened by the forced Syrian withdrawal from Lebanon and the threats of external intervention coming from Washington. However, as Ikhwani hopes for regime change in Damascus progressively died down, it became "embarrassing"[53] for the Brotherhood to remain associated with a former prominent Ba'athist figure who had participated in the massacre of its own members. In January 2009, Ikhwani leaders suspended their opposition activities, officially in order to show support for the Syrian regime's popular anti-Israel stance during the war in Gaza. "While we, the Muslim Brotherhood, sided with the people of Gaza who were defending themselves, Khaddam was blaming Hamas for the escalation of violence and refused to freeze his opposition to Assad for the duration of the war",[54] explains Ali Sadreddine al-Bayanouni. This, however, was described as a "mere pretext"[55] by Abdel Halim Khaddam, who claims that the real reason behind the Brotherhood's withdrawal from the NSF was in fact an Ikhwani willingness to negotiate its way back to Damascus with the Syrian regime. This is confirmed by Obeida Nahas, according to whom a "mediation" between the Ikhwani leadership and the Ba'athist rulers indeed took place sometime between 2009 and 2010, although he insists that "the talks never moved beyond the mediation phase".[56]

The "return of the Hamawites" and the "Arab Spring": a new way forward?

Despite the Brotherhood's failure to negotiate its way back to Syria, Ali Sadreddine al-Bayanouni's three tenures at the helm of the Ikhwan proved successful insofar as he put the exiled organization back into the media spotlight. At the same time, however, many of the initiatives he took proved controversial, from the alliance with Khaddam to the decision of initiating a mediation with the regime. Here again, the ideological divisions within the movement mostly overlapped with geographical lines. "By 1991-1992, the Hamawites had come back into the fold of the Muslim Brotherhood. Ever since, they have projected Adnan Saadeddine's political vision into the movement even though he was not himself included in the merger",[57] explains Zouheir Salem, the artisan of the Ikhwan's moderation and a long-time member of the "Aleppo faction". The Hamawite Farouk Tayfour, Bayanouni's deputy at the head of the organization, was especially vocal in his criticism of the way in which the Aleppine leader handled the movement during his three terms. When, in July 2010, elections were held inside the movement to decide on a new leader for the organization, the candidate put forward by the "Hama clan", Muhammed Riyadh al-Shuqfah, was elected.

The leadership change carried with it a charged symbolic value as the "Hama clan" had not been in charge of the whole organization since the bloody events of the late 1970s. It had also been the target of criticism by many inside the movement, who blamed some of its members for having pushed the Brotherhood into the ill-fated violent confrontation with the regime. Their return to the height of the Syrian Ikhwan's leadership therefore inspired several alarmist comments on the possibility that the "return of the Hamawites" could signal an ideological shift putting into question Bayanouni's moderate legacy.[58] Some moderate sympathizers of the organization even called Shuqfah's election a "setback" for the Islamic movement. Upon taking his function, the new leader asserted that the Muslim Brotherhood would immediately resume its opposition activities against the Syrian Ba'ath, the truce with the regime having for him ended the day the Gaza war did.[59] At first, the ideologically more hard-line stance taken by Shuqfah seems to have been coupled by an attempt from the "Hama clan" to marginalize the "Aleppo faction" long in charge of the Ikhwan. Prominent Aleppine Ikhwanis such as Ali Sadreddine al-Bayanouni, Obeida Nahas and Zouheir Salem were sidelined. Once again, ideological and geographical fault lines seemed to overlap.

Aware that the increasingly visible divisions plaguing the Islamic movement would eventually hurt its credibility as a sustainable opposition force, the new Hamawite leadership called back in the "Aleppo faction" after sensing that Bashar al-Assad could be next in line after popular protests of the "Arab Spring" had toppled Tunisia's Ben Ali and Egypt's Mubarrak. In March 2011, Zouheir Salem was asked to become the Ikhwan's spokesman and, shortly afterwards, Ali Sadreddine al-Bayanouni accepted to act as Muhammed Riyadh al-Shuqfah's "special adviser". It also seems as if, with the advent of the "Arab Spring", much of the ideological divide pitting the "Hama clan" against the "Aleppo faction" has been bridged. The fierce repression suffered by anti-regime demonstrators at the hands of the state's security apparatus has rendered irrelevant calls to negotiate with a Ba'athist regime now seen as wholly illegitimate. In addition, the regime's denunciations of the demonstrations as a "plot against Syria" carried out by the Muslim Brotherhood and supported by foreigners seem to have, ironically, increased the organization's internal cohesiveness and common sense of purpose. Doctrinally, the two wings of the Ikhwan seem to have been similarly influenced by the "Turkish example", which they both cite as their model in a post-Bashar, Ikhwani-dominated Syria. "We are impressed by the Turkish governance system and we are not keen on the Iranian model as we don't want to impose anything on the people",[60] Shuqfah recently declared in an interview. While the Syrian Ikhwan is not new to parliamentary democracy, having contested elections throughout the 1950s and early 1960s, the Islamist AK Party ruling Turkey has provided Syria's Muslim Brotherhood with a blueprint for reform. "The AKP is neutral in the area of religion – neither does it impose religion upon its citizens nor does it seek to fight religion – and for this reason we find it to be an excellent model",[61] Bayanouni for his part declared. Of course, there are still disagreements inside the organization, most notably on the form taken by a possible "international protection" of the Syrian protestors and on the extent to which the Ikhwan should compromise on its principles while participating to the activities of the opposition in exile. However, much of the debate on armed struggle which, in the 1980s, used to oppose the two wings of the movement has now withered. Early on during the protests, prominent members of both the "Aleppo faction" and the "Hama group" have reiterated with insistence their rejection of violence as a means to confront the regime. While Ali Sadreddine al-Bayanouni emphasized the importance of using "non-violent means"[62] to overthrow the Assad regime, Muhammed Riyadh al-Shuqfah insisted for his part on "the peacefulness of the revolution". Commenting on the role of the "Free Syria Army", the leader of the Ikhwan went as far as warning against civilians joining the armed umbrella group:

> "The soldiers who defected from the regular army are defending themselves against this army. The self-defence of the dissidents is a legitimate right, but it is unacceptable for the people to join. Several groups of demonstrating youths asked us whether they should join the dissidents and we told them no. We caution the people against becoming involved in military action".[63]

At first glance, Shuqfah's comments can be seen as surprising as the Hamawites' historical advocacy of the necessity to confront the Syrian Ba'ath with arms, if needed, has become an increasingly popular demand inside Syria. The "Hama group", however, as well as the broader Muslim Brotherhood organization, have over the past two decades undergone a profound ideological change towards more moderation when it comes to the issue of the means employed to oppose the Syrian Ba'ath. That "the Muslim Brotherhood has changed"[64] is also recognized by Burhan Ghalioun, a long-time left-wing member of the exiled opposition who now acts as head of the Syrian National Council (SNC).

Since March 2011, the multiplication of anti-regime protests in Syria has pushed the exiled opposition to present a more unified stance to both the international community and the Syrian protesters. The Muslim Brotherhood has been a key driver behind the organization of a series of conferences held by Syrian opposition groups outside the country. Observers have sometimes expressed surprise at the high turnout and visibility of the movement during recent opposition meetings held in Antalya, Brussels and Istanbul.[65] The Ikhwan, for its part, has been keen on insisting that it is "a supporter, not a creator"[66] of the uprisings which have sprung up throughout Syria over the past year. Internally, the movement claims that the Syrian protesters have no links to the Ikhwan even though it suggests that many of them are sympathizers.[67] Externally, the organization strives to fully cooperate with secular left-wing dissidents, Kurdish parties and independent groups in order to more effectively coordinate opposition activities.

When asked about its influence in the exiled opposition's main political body, the Syrian National Council (SNC), its leader assures that the Ikhwan does not have, contrarily to what some suggest, control over it.[68] This willingness to downplay the movement's newfound influential role should not be seen as surprising, given the fact that many inside and outside Syria continue to associate the Muslim Brotherhood with the violence which struck the country in the late 1970s and early 1980s.

However, despite its cautiousness not to take any visible leadership role in the current protests inside and outside Syria, the Ikhwani leadership is well-aware of the Muslim Brotherhood's strength. Zouheir Salem, the Ikhwan's spokesman, has suggested that well over half of the forces making-up the exiled opposition are related in one way or another to the Islamic movement.[69] If such an estimate may be slightly exaggerated, one cannot dismiss the fact that the Syrian Muslim Brotherhood is, to date, the most organized and best funded of all opposition forces, as even its rivals admit.[70] According to Zouheir Salem, this is due to the "extraordinary ideological commitment" and "resilience"[71] which Ikhwani members have shown over the past decades. Despite being scattered throughout the world since the early 1980s, the movement seems to have retained much of its institutional and organizational capacity. Today, the emergence of a new generation of younger and moderate Ikhwani leaders who have almost always lived in exile, such as Moulhem al-Droubi, Obeida Nahas or Ahmed al-Ramadan, seems to suggest that the old geographical and ideological divisions, which have plagued the movement's ranks for a long time, may soon become a thing of the past.

For long, the Syrian Islamic landscape has tended to boil down solely to the Muslim Brotherhood. Since the advent of mass anti-regime protests after March 2011, new actors have nevertheless emerged with the aim of ultimately contesting the Ikhwan's prominent place on the political chessboard both outside and inside Syria. Some argue that, inside the country, the *Ulama* ("religious scholars") are best positioned to increase their political influence in a post-Assad Syria. However, the men of religion are divided between those who have been co-opted by the Ba'ath regime, in which they have a vested interest, and those who have lent their support to the Syrian protesters.[72] Others argue that, outside Syria, the London-based Movement for Justice and Development (MJD) is increasingly acting as an efficient political and ideological challenger to the Muslim Brotherhood's hegemony over the opposition in exile. Malik al-Abdeh, the co-founder of the MJD, described in an interview the "turf war"[73] which opposes his political platform to the Islamic organization. Explicitly created as a more modern and moderate outlet than the Ikhwan, the MJD has, however, tended to act more as a network than as a political party and it has been hurt by revelations last spring that parts of its activities had been financed by bodies depending upon US government funding.[74] Despite the long exile into which it has been forced since 1982 and the numerous divisions which have arisen ever since, the Muslim Brotherhood therefore seems to remain the most cohesive and best organized force in the landscape of Syrian Islamic politics.

Overall, the Ikhwan's historic role of resistance to the Syrian Ba'ath – and the heavy price it has paid for it – gives the Islamic organization a particular legitimacy to act as a prominent actor in Syrian politics. In return for its opposition, however, the Muslim Brotherhood's recent history has been mostly shaped by the troubled relationship it has entertained ever since the late 1970s with a Ba'athist regime willing to exploit the organization's inherent contradictions in order to "divide and rule". While the Ikhwan flirted with the violent option during the late 1970s and early 1980s, it mellowed its discourse and its tactics throughout the 1990s and 2000s, hoping it could eventually be allowed to return to Syria in order to rebuild the political capability it once had at the grassroots level. Its mediation efforts having proved unsuccessful, it entered into various opposition coalitions with other political forces –a feature which continues to dominate the Muslim Brotherhood's mindset to this day as it increasingly seems to act as the most influential actor of exiled Syrian politics.

---

[1] "Assad : challenge Syria at your peril", *Daily Telegraph*, 29/10/2011.

[2] Olivier Carré and Gérard Michaud, *Les Frères Musulmans (1928-1982)*, (Gallimard, Paris 1983), p. 134.

[3] Ikhwani member Muhammad al-Mubarak quoted in Nazih Ayoubi, *Political Islam: religion and politics in the Arab world* (Routledge, New York, 1991), p. 89.

[4] Interview with Abdel Halim Khaddam, Paris, 23/6/2011.

[5] For more information on the advent of the "neo-Ba'ath" and its policies, see : Gordon Torrey, "The Neo-Ba'ath : ideology and practice", *Middle East Journal* (Vol. 23, No. 4, 1969).

[6] See: *Al-Nadhir*, No. 1, September 6th, 1979 and No. 6, 8th November, 1979, quoted in Nikolaos Van Dam *The Struggle for power in Syria: politics and society under Asad and the Ba'th Party* (I.B. Tauris and Co. Ltd, London, 2011, 4th Edition), p. 90.

[7] Interviews with Ali Sadreddine al-Bayanouni, London, 30/11/2011; Muhammed Hawari, Aachen, 19/11/2011; Zouheir Salem, London, 3/6/2011; Muhammed Riyad al-Shuqfah, Istanbul, 9/9/2011; Issam al-Attar, Aachen, 19/11/2011. For more on the split between the "Damascus wing" and the "Northern axis", see my forthcoming book: *Ashes of Hama: the troubled fate of Syria's Muslim Brotherhood* (Hurst & Co, London, 2012).

[8] Umar Faruk Abd Allah, *The Islamic struggle in Syria* (Mizan Press, Berkley, 1983), p. 102.

[9] The "Qutbist" thought refers to prominent Egyptian Brother ideologue Sayyid Qutb who, in his 1964 pamphlet entitled *Ma'alim fi'l Tariq* ("Signs on the road"), advocated armed struggle against Arab regimes considered as "impious" or "non-Islamic" –such as Nasser's Egypt and Ba'athist Syria. To reach this goal, Qutb argued that a "vanguard" of "enlightened Muslims" should take matters inside their hands and directly target the most prominent symbols of such regimes. For more information on Sayyid Qutb and his ideological influence upon contemporary Islamic movements, see: Nazih Ayubi, *Political Islam: religion and politics* (Routledge, New York, 1991).

[10] Interview with Ali Sadreddine al-Bayanouni, London, 30/11/2011.

[11] Interview with Zouheir Salem, London, 3/10/2011.

[12] Interview with Muhammed Riyad al-Shuqfah, Istanbul, 9/9/2011.

[13] Interview with Walid Safour, London, 22/9/2011.

[14] Interview with Muhammed Hawari, Aachen, 19/11/2011.

[15] Interview with Zouheir Salem, London, 20/7/2011.

[16] For a detailed account of the Hama massacre resting on testimonies from survivors, see: James A. Paul, *Syria unmasked: the suppression of human rights by the Asad regime* (Middle East Watch and Yale University Press, Yale, 1991), pp. 18-21.

[17] Interview with Muhammed Riyad al-Shuqfah, Istanbul, 9/9/2011.

[18] Interview with Zouheir Salem, London, 20/7/2011.

[19] Interview with Ali Sadreddine al-Bayanouni, London, 30/11/2011.

[20] Interview with Muhammed Riyad al-Shuqfah, Istanbul, 9/9/2011.

[21] Adnan Saadeddine quoted in Alison Pargeter, *The Muslim Brotherhood: the burden of tradition* (Saqi Books, London, 2010) p. 85.

[22] Adnan Saadeddine quote in Hanna Batatu, p. 269.

[23] Interview with Muhammed Riyad al-Shuqfah, Istanbul, 9/9/2011.

[24] Adnan Saadeddine, *Mesirat jama'at al-ikhwan al-Muslimeen fi Suria* (Private publisher, July 1998). See Alison Pargeter, *The Muslim Brotherhood: the burden of tradition* (Saqi Books, London, 2010), pp. 85-87.

[25] Interview with Muhammed Riyad al-Shuqfah, Istanbul, 9/9/2011.

[26] Interview with Abdel Halim Khaddam, Paris, 23/6/2011.

[27] Interview with Issam al-Attar, Aachen, 19/11/2011.

[28] Interview with Muhammed Riyad al-Shuqfah, Istanbul, 9/9/2011.

[29] Interview with Walid Safour, London, 22/9/2011.

[30] Interview with Muhammed Riyad al-Shuqfah, Istanbul, 9/9/2011.

[31] Interview with Abdel Halim Khaddam, Paris, 23/6/2011.

[32] Adnan Saadeddine quoted in Chris Kutchera, "Wither the Syrian Muslim Brothers", *Middle East Magazine* (April 1988), available online at: http://www.chris-kutschera.com/A/syrian_brothers.htm.

[33] Interview with Muhammed Riyad al-Shuqfah, Istanbul, 9/9/2011.

[34] Interview with Zouheir Salem, London, 9/9/2011.

[35] Ali Duba quoted in Chris Kutschera, "Syrie: l'éclipse des Frères Musulmans", *Cahiers de l'Orient* (No. 7, Volume 3, 1987), also available online at : http://www.chris-kutschera.com/syrie_eclipse_fm.htm.

[36] Interview with Ali Sadreddine al-Bayanouni, London, 30/11/2011.

[37] Interview with Muhammed Riyad al-Shuqfah, Istanbul, 9/9/2011.
[38] Interview with Obeida Nahas, London, 30/6/2011.
[39] Chris Kutschera, "Syrie: l'éclipse des Frères Musulmans", *Cahiers de l'Orient* (No. 7, Volume 3, 1987), also available online at : http://www.chris-kutschera.com/syrie_eclipse_fm.htm.
[40] Interview with Zouheir Salem, London, 2/10/2011.
[41] See: *The political perspective for Syria: the Muslim Brotherhood's vision of the future* (London, December 2004, copy given to the author), pp. 3-4 and *The National Charter of Syria* (London, August 2002, copy given to the author), p. 6.
[42] Interview with Zouheir Salem, London, 20/7/2011.
[43] Interview with Zouheir Salem, London, 20/7/2011.
[44] *US Embassy cable to State Department*, "The Syrian Muslim Brotherhood" (DAMASCUS 575, 26th February 1985), available at: http://wikileaks.org/cable/1985/02/85DAMASCUS1314.html.
[45] The estimate of 10,000 prisoners suspected of belonging to the Muslim Brotherhood comes from a spokesman of al-Talia al-Muqatila, quoted in *US Embassy cable to State Department*, "The Syrian Muslim Brotherhood" (DAMASCUS 575, 26th February 1985). For the figures related to Hafiz al-Assad's release of political prisoners, see: Eyal Zisser, "Syria, the Baath regime and the Islamic movement : stepping on a new path ?", *The Muslim World* (Vol. 95, No. 1, 2005), p. 49.
[46] Eyal Zisser, *op. cit.*, p. 52.
[47] Interview with Muhammed Riyad al-Shuqfah, Istanbul, 9/9/2011.
[48] Eyal Zisser, *op. cit.*, p. 55.
[49] Joshua Landis, "The Syrian opposition : the struggle for unity and relevance, 2003-2008" in Fred H. Lawson (ed.), *Demistifying Syria* (Saqi Books, London 2009), p. 129.
[50] Interview with Abdel Halim Khaddam, Paris, 23/6/2011.
[51] Interview with Obeida Nahas, London 23/6/2011.
[52] "Khaddam's and Bayanouni's Faustian pact", *US Embassy in Damascus' cable to State Department* (C-NE6-00262, 18/4/2006).
[53] Interview with Obeida Nahas, London, 23/6/2011.
[54] Interviews with Ali Sadreddine al-Bayanouni, London, 30/11/2011.
[55] Interview with Abdel Halim Khaddam, Paris, 23/6/2011.
[56] Interview with Obeida Nahas, London, 23/6/2011.
[57] Interview with Zouheir Salem, London, 20/7/2011.
[58] See, for instance, Najib Ghadbian, "Syria's Muslim Brothers: where to next?", *Daily Star* (17/9/2010).
[59] "New Syrian Brotherhood leader announces an end to truce with regime", *al-Masry al-Youm*, 13/8/2010.
[60] "Syria's Muslim Brotherhood favors Turkey over Iran in plan for power", *Bloomberg*, 28/11/2011.
[61] Piotr Zalewski, "Islamic evolution", *Foreign Policy*, 11/8/2011.
[62] Ali al-Bayanuni, "No one owns Syria's uprisings", *Guardian* (16/4/2011).
[63] "Asharq al-Awsat talks to Syria's Muslim Brotherhood leader", *Asharq al-Awsat*, 11/10/2010.

[64] Interview with Burhan Ghalioun, Paris, 2/6/2011.
[65] "Syrian opposition unites in exile", *Washington Post* (2/6/2011).
[66] Zouheir Salem quoted in "Brotherhood raises Syria profile", *Wall Street Journal* (17/5/2011).
[67] Interview with Zouheir Salem, London, 20/7/2011.
[68] "Syria's Muslim Brotherhood favors Turkey over Iran in plan for power", *Bloomberg*, 28/11/2011, available at: http://www.bloomberg.com/news/2011-11-28/syria-s-muslim-brotherhood-favors-turkish-model-over-iran-s-leader-says.html.
[69] Interview with Zouheir Salem, London, 20/7/2011.
[70] Fadwa al-Halem, "A new opposition for Syria", *The Guardian* (7/6/2011).
[71] Interview with Zouheir Salem, London, 20/7/2011.
[72] For an excellent analysis of the role played by Syrian Ulama in the current protests, see: Thomas Pierret, "Syrie: l'Islam dans la revolution", *Politique Etrangère* (Vol. 4, 2011), pp. 879-891.
[73] Interview with Malik el-Abdeh, London, 6/12/2011.
[74] "Movement for Justice and Development seeking to expand role in Syria", *US Embassy in Damascus' cable to State Department* (DE RUEHDM 00185, 11/3/2011), also see: "Murky alliances: Muslim Brotherhood, the Movement for Justice and Democracy and the Damascus Declaration", *US Embassy in Damascus' cable to State Department* (DE RUEHDN 000477, 8/7/2009), available at: http://www.washingtonpost.com/wp-srv/special/world/wikileaks-syria/cable4.html.

2
Islamic Revival and the Promotion of Moderate Islam from Above[1]

Line Khatib

Introduction

Syria has witnessed a number of profound changes over the last 20 years or so that have fundamentally reshaped the country's political and socio-economic landscape. The most important of these changes include a selective liberalization of the economy, which has caused the gap between the rich and the poor to widen as well as led to the re-emergence of a Syrian oligarchy after years of populist public policy in the country. Just as important has been a clear and palpable religious revivalism,[2] one that is condoned by the regime, this despite the fact that the regime's system of authoritarian rule is supposedly secular and moreover bans the politicization of religion. As a result of these changes, political and economic power are being increasingly concentrated in the hands of a few families, while a number of Islamic religious leaders now wield significant social influence.

The organizations led by the religious leaders are invariably pietistic in nature rather than politically oriented. This is a direct result of the regime's struggle against a radical Islamic opposition during the late 1970s, which culminated in the Hama massacre of 1982 in which the country's most powerful Islamic actor, the Muslim Brotherhood, was crushed. In the aftermath of that struggle, the regime co-opted, and later accommodated and empowered, the apolitical Islamic organizations that remained.[3] Today, a number of these Islamic populist Sufi groups have become prominent parts of the Syrian social landscape. And while some are more modernist than others, they are all similar in their adoption of an agenda that is more concerned with charitable work and the *da'wa* (proselytizing) to Islam rather than being focused upon becoming part of the political apparatus, or indeed on any form of overt political engagement. The efforts of these groups are a major reason for the increased number of Islamized spaces in Syria today, in terms of more conservative attire, more widespread Islamic practices, a greater number of Islamic bookstores – which barely existed in the 1980s and early 1990s – and greater production and consumption of Islamic literature.[4] In highlighting this change, it is simultaneously important to underline that the "Islamizing" mechanisms of charitable work and *da'wa* used by the Syrian Sufi orders are not new, nor are they foreign imports. Apolitical members of the Muslim Brothers, who had reservations regarding militant activism and confronting the state, earlier advanced the notion that the gradual re-creation of Islamized spaces within the secular public sphere would provide the necessary supportive environment for greater Islamization of Syrian society.[5]

While these trends within Syrian society are supported by some citizens, they are increasingly worrisome to others. Many of the latter look to the fall of secular Baathism in Iraq and the ensuing factionalism and religious violence as a portent of what might happen in Syria. As a result, old fears and battles regarding the country's secular and socially pluralist heritage, and, more fundamentally, the Islamist question itself are now resurfacing.[6] From the point of view of Syrian secularists, there have been strong concerns that what is left of the Syrian secular environment was being dismantled,[7] which they argued would eventually undermine the country's ideological, ethnic and religious diversity.[8] Furthermore, according to pro-democracy activists, the regime's empowerment and accommodation of these groups was proof of a conscious and divisive manipulation of Syrian society, one that could only have negative consequences in the longer term.

Thus, the country presently faces a situation in which many Syrians have joined the piety movement and are consequently supporting and contributing to Syria's Islamic revival while many others have emphatically rejected it, frequently by making reference to the "manipulative" and "foreign" origins of certain Islamic trends. It is in light of this palpable revival and the widening cleavages that it is provoking in Syrian society that an ostensibly alarmed regime sought to reverse these trends, with a verbal decree in 2010 banning around 1,000 *munaqabat* women (women with a full-face veil) from teaching.[9] A few days later, *munaqabat* women were also banned from registering as students at the university level.[10] This latter decision by the state has been interpreted by observers as underlining the tension between the government's wish to retain Syria's Islamic environment under control and its expressed willingness[11] to condone a rising Islamic movement as part of a pro-regime civil society. Complicating this dilemma still further is the regime's own crucial role in encouraging and facilitating the Islamic revival. It did so as part of an "authoritarian upgrading" that necessitated reinventing Syria's Islamic discourse while at the same time closing off the country's intellectual, civic, and political space to what was seen as the greatest challenge to its own political hegemony, the Syrian pro-democracy movement.

The objective of this paper is twofold. First, to analyse how Syria's Islamic religious movement engineered its own rebirth in the 1980s and 1990s under an authoritarian regime that was ostensibly secular and thus by definition hostile to public religiosity, including giving consideration to the role of the regime itself in this process. The second part of the paper aims to shed light on how the Syrian state dealt with the Islamic movement's rising popular legitimacy and influence up to the end of 2010. This section will also look at the reactions of Syrian society to the increasing influence of Islamic groups. One conclusion will be affirmed throughout: the Syrian piety movement grew in general increasingly powerful under a state that enabled it, to the point that the movement shifted from being a client of the state to being its powerful ally, and may now be turning into an enemy.

Syria's Islamic Revival: State-Manufactured and Controlled

The state's need to ensure a new Islamic discourse and movement in Syria became evident in the late 1970s as the traditional Islamic discourse was political and thus unwelcomed by the Baathist rulers. The traditional Islamic movement had arguably been unified under the Muslim Brothers in the late 1930s and early 1940s, enjoying some influence within Syrian society and, perhaps more importantly, playing a constructive role within the country's political life by taking part in what were then free parliamentary elections. Indeed, they even managed to win a few seats in the parliament against their more popular liberal and leftist rivals. But this political space that the Islamist groups enjoyed was shut down by Jamal Abd al-Nasser at the time of the creation of the United Arab Republic between Syria and Egypt in 1958 (as it was for all political parties under the new regime). This closed political realm became even more hostile to opposition groups in 1963 with the 8th of March Baathi coup.

The effect of the closing off of political participation was to give impetus to the notion – already more or less latent within the Islamic movement – that militancy, as a defence mechanism against the authoritarian regime, was necessary in order to reassert some of the Brothers' lost social and political influence. Thus the movement started challenging the regime, and those challenges ultimately grew into a widespread uprising in the late 1970s and early 1980s. Yet the uprising, which also included leftist and Nasserist opposition groups, failed to oust the Ba'thist regime. Part of the reason for its failure were internal divisions within the Islamic movement, coupled with the active measures taken by the regime to safeguard its rule. These regime measures included: 1) from the 1970s onwards, broadening its ruling coalition to include the business class and a pacifist religious class, thereby incorporating into the coalition elements of the socio-economic elite who had up until then lost out significantly under the populist authoritarian Baathi regime; 2) launching a concerted attack against its secularist opponents and eventually dismantling any viable pro-democratic alternative to Baathi rule, leftist or otherwise; and 3) shrinking the elements of institutional power still available to and controlled by the anti-regime Islamists through a process that involved dismantling and appropriating the country's religious institutions, which in turn allowed the state to achieve significant control over the religious discourse within the country. Regarding the first measure, the inclusion of pacifist and apolitical religious leaders able to attract large urban audiences, including several who would later become some of Syria's most prominent shaykhs, "helped put an end to political Islam in Syria, while also ensuring the survival and later expansion of a renewed politically quietist Islamic movement."[12]

The manner in which the regime dealt with the militant opposition protests from the seventies onward played a significant role in redefining Syria ideologically, socially and politically. In addition to the measures taken by the regime to safeguard its rule (described above), it adopted a variety of survival strategies that included muting Syrian secularism and politically co-opting the religious class through an accommodation and an enabling of those religious shaykhs who were willing to become part of the state's crony network. Therefore, the Islamic revival that Syria witnessed in the 1990s is effectively rooted in the state's responses to the earlier Islamist and secularist challenge to its authoritarian rule.[13] Moreover its character – in terms of being an Islamic renewal that has focused on *da'wa*, Islamic practice, and a discreet and gradual Islamization of entire sub-communities within Syria's cities – was similarly shaped by the state's responses.

In emphasizing the regime's key role in both tolerating and facilitating the powerful Islamic resurgence, it is simultaneously important to recognize the agency of Syria's shaykhs in successfully adapting to their changing circumstances. For instance, the shaykhs managed to spread their influence to a new membership of younger recruits that had once been attracted to the secular revolutionary groups. This underlines their effective reading of, and pragmatic response to, the non-political opportunity structures with which the Assad regime presented them. As part of their coping mechanisms, the shaykhs drew upon their firm grounding in orthodoxy to initiate a program of Islamic regeneration that was hailed by one of the country's largest Islamic groups as the dawn of an Islamic *Renaissance* - *"Bidayat al-Fath al-Jadid"* [the start of the new victory].[14] Their ability to carry out the program of Islamic regeneration was certainly made easier by "the strategy of Hafez al-Asad's regime of shifting the conflict from one between the Muslim Brothers and a corrupt ruling clique to one between 'moderate good Muslims' and 'radical terrorist Muslims'..."[15] Within this new regime-defined dichotomy, the shaykhs constituted the leaders of the "moderate good Muslims", whose discourse and actions stood in marked contrast to that of the marginalized and persecuted anti-regime Islamists. Yet the flip side of the regime's favouring of the Islamic sector is that the secularist intelligentsia were no longer able to effectively spread their message; largely as a result of being unable to assemble due to the strictures imposed by Syria's emergency law and the concomitant fact that they did not have the advantage available to the religious sector of being able to meet in mosques and churches. This of course has had important longer-term repercussions for the secular element within Syrian society.

The era of Bashar al-Assad, which began in June 2000, can be considered critical in the growth of Islamic groups. This is because the new president continued his father's policy of co-optation and accommodation of the groups. More particularly, the son sought to buttress his legitimacy in as part of a strategy of coping with the "Damascus Spring" (2000-2001) which witnessed the reinvigoration of a myriad of opposition secular groups that had been dormant under the regime of Hafiz al-Assad by deepening and reinforcing his interaction with old and new Islamic clients. Indeed, as soon as he inherited power, Bashar al-Assad announced that there was a moral need – and, while not explicitly stated, likely a strategic need as well – to officially[16] open a new phase of relations with Syria's Islamic movement, one based on accommodation and dialogue.[17] To that end, the president promoted the ideas of *"takrees al-akhlaq wa nashr thaqafat al-tasamuh, wa isal al-risala al-haqiqiya lil-islam"* [diffusing morality, spreading the culture of tolerance, and communicating the true message of Islam - author's translation] in many of his addresses, interviews and conference presentations.[18] The new phase of relations was subsequently marked by Bashar al-Assad committing his government to becoming a patron of moderate Islam. This was done in the name of "national unity," "moderation" and "countering the rising wave of Islamic radicalism (*al-Tataruf*)".[19] In so doing, his regime effectively legitimized the Islamic discourse engulfing the country.

The state's accommodationist stance was marked by a number of social and political decrees that appeared to be both symbolically and practically conciliatory toward the Islamic sector. One of them involved the repeal in 2000 of a 1982 decree prohibiting the wearing of Islamic headscarves by girls and women in any part of the country's educational system.[20] This move was seen as symbolically significant, in spite of the fact that the decree had not been enforced since 1982.[21] In addition, Bashar al-Assad's regime allowed many of those who were in political exile to return safely to Syria, including some opposition figures who were members of Syria's Muslim Brothers, such as Abu Fateh al-Bayanuni, the brother of the Syrian Muslim Brotherhood's leader 'Ali Ṣadr al-Din al-Bayanuni. Long-serving prisoners accused of belonging to Islamic groups, some of whom had been in prison for 20 years, were released from prison. These included some 800 Muslim Brotherhood political prisoners, among them senior Islamic leaders such as Khalid al-Shami, who was one of the leaders of the Islamic uprising against the regime in the 1970s and who had been in the infamous Tadmur prison since 1982.[22] The regime also closed down the notorious Mezza military prison on 13 September 2000, which had become a symbol of the regime's cruel repression of political dissidents, a majority of whom were Islamists.[23] The message that the new command seemed to be sending was that the Syrian political landscape was shifting and that old battles need no longer continue to be fought.

The Syrian leadership also started incorporating Islam more overtly into state institutions. For instance, in February 2004 the Syrian state organized the country's first "religious" conference in 40 years. And in 2006, the military academy, long known for its radically secular environment and sometimes overt disregard for religious sensibilities, invited religious authorities to lecture cadets for the first time since the Baath's rise to power in 1963. Those invited included Syria's Mufti Ahmad Hassoun, MP Shaykh Ahmad Habash and Christian Patriarch Isidor Batikha, all of who spoke on the role of religion in confronting the new geopolitical challenges faced by the Syrian nation.[24] The visit underlined the leadership's willingness to openly use religious discourse to influence its citizenry, something that had not been done by Assad the father. The regime's increasing embrace of religion also led to new shaykhs being recruited to official Islamic institutions and by the Ministry of Endowments.

Other significant moves made by the government included turning a blind eye to the overwhelming number of Syrians joining Islamic groups and taking Islamic lessons inside and outside mosques. Indeed, Syrians were allowed and even encouraged to organize public religious festivals and to post religious banners in the streets in celebration of religious events – whether Christian or Muslim – something that had not been seen in Damascus for decades.[25] For many Syrians, the prominent displaying of such banners on the streets of the country's cities was striking given the once implicit prohibition on such symbols in the public realm.

Furthermore, an increased number of prominent Islamic figures competed for seats in the Syrian "People's Assembly" or parliament. Thus the most recent legislative elections involved many "independents" who were either religious figures or known businessmen associated with a religious leader. Pierret and Selvik explain that in the 2007 legislative elections, "Muhammad Hamshu, a nouveau-riche Sunni and crony of the Assad family, and 'Abd al-Salam Rajih, dean of Kaftaru Academy's shari'a faculty, came out on top with about 80,000 votes each."[26] It is important to underline that these are not members of the opposition Islamic movement, but are rather part of the state-approved Islamic movement. A further observation is that these figures' strong performance in parliamentary elections shows that the state's tolerance of them is matched by their popular support within the Syrian electorate.

Some observers have argued that the state's accommodation of the Islamic sector at the social and political levels was due to its need to minimize the destabilizing effects of the war in neighbouring Iraq that began in 2003– such as refugee flows into Syria – as well as the fallout from the assassination of Lebanese President Rafiq Hariri in February 2005, which Syria was accused of having a hand in. But the above analysis has shown that it actually preceded these events, and that it was an outgrowth of the need to reconfigure state-society relations in order to maintain the unity of the ruling coalition and to ensure the regime's survival well before these external challenges. At the same time, this reconfiguration was not necessarily as smooth as the regime would have liked it to be. As we will see in the next section of the chapter, the ways in which these shaykhs and their groups rapidly grew over the following years would become increasingly relevant to understandings and analyses of Syrian politics in the future. And while it is impossible to predict the future – particularly within a dynamic setting like today's Syria – it is clear that the reconfigurations of the country's social landscape will ultimately have an impact upon its politics.

Islam in Contemporary Syria

As we have seen, the shaykhs who wished to continue their work acquiesced to the political regime, some more willingly than others. They thereby demonstrated their realization that the continuation of the Islamic project meant an overt and fundamental disengagement from the world of politics, due to the controls imposed by Syria's authoritarian political setting. At the same time, the economic and political co-optation undertaken by the Hafez al-Assad regime was also a powerful incentive for a number of shaykhs within the religious movement to acquiesce to its demands.[27]

Political Abstention

Practically speaking, disengaging from politics has meant that Islamic shaykhs advanced a social and an ethical agenda, one that aimed at the moral reform of individuals and groups and focused on transforming the sub-communal levels of society. This is a far cry from political Islam's typical focus on the re-organization of society by wielding the powers of the state.[28] As a result of this disengagement from politics, many of the most prominent and recurring themes in the shaykhs' discourse and writings have focused entirely on the individual, on questions such as: what does it mean to be a true Muslim, what does religious ethicality mean, how does one practice his/her faith, what does compassion and tolerance mean in Islam, and how should one deal with divergences of opinion amongst Muslims. Their literature was both personalized and popularist.[29] This means that people were encouraged to be actively involved in their own religiosity by spreading the message of Islam and of the movement, and by participating in and publicizing the movement's activities. Pamphlets distributed in mosques, as well as more widely available books and magazines, underlined that the duty of every Muslim to promote the "right Islam" begins with a change from within, rendered as a *Fard 'Ayn* (religious obligation incumbent upon the individual in Islam). Islamic micro-communities were created and presented as "liberated zones" in which the "formation of the Spiritual Muslim" (*al-Islam wa Bina' al-Insan al-Rabbani*)[30] was possible, something that was characterized as being in the best interests of the individual *and* society because it is only when a person commits himself to complete obedience to God that he will be able to cultivate the seeds of social justice and righteous living.

How do Islamic groups capture the hearts and minds of Syrians? Part of the way that they do so is by undertaking extensive ideological outreach, outreach that is rendered more potent by virtue of its unitary message that is continuously repeated to persuade the public and that gains further impetus because it is the only message besides that of the regime's that is allowed in the public sphere. At the same time, funds arriving from the Gulf region, welfare associations, the provision of social services and *volontariat* work helped to bolster the Islamic groups' capacity to recruit new members. And although the groups' social activism encompassed the entirety of society, it particularly targeted young people, with efforts made to entice them into joining the social network and remaining within its zone of influence. This is because the preponderance of young people in the country (more than 50% of the population is under the age of 30) makes them a key target demographically whose support is necessary since it can provide the Islamic groups with the numbers and thus ultimately a significant amount of power within society.

As mentioned earlier, ideological framing has been an essential part of the recruiting process aimed at young people. The Islamic groups have also worked to address the youths' socio-economic problems and needs, through charitable work, by undertaking social activities of all sorts as well as by providing free educational and employment programs. The impact of these programs has been made even greater as a result of the fact that the Syrian regime was simultaneously been gradually reducing the state's welfare functions. Indeed, instead of continuing to cater to the middle classes and lower classes, the newly embourgeoised political elite that inexorably emerged as a result of the formerly populist authoritarian regime's neo-liberal policies instead pushed for more economic liberalization. Yet this economic liberalization is a purported policy aim rather than actual widespread practice, with its benefits tending to accrue based on who one knows and bribes paid to officials; it has thus tended to disproportionately benefit the elite and crony capitalists at the expense of the middle and lower middle classes in the country. Most disadvantaged of all have been the Syrian youth, a fact which has made them even more ripe targets for the Islamic outreach efforts described above.

Implications of Islamic Social Activism
It is important to note that, although the Islamic outreach was made more palatable to the wider Syrian public as a result of its ostensibly apolitical nature, the Islamic message put forth by the official Islamic groups certainly does take political stances. For instance, it insists that the core Islamic message is about fairness, human compassion and morality rather than political power, a vision that religiously justifies the closing of the political realm to full participation.[31] Relatedly, shaykhs

have argued for accepting the authority of the state regardless of its ideology and its actions. They have done so by emphasizing the importance within the Islamic historical and institutional tradition of working with *de facto* political authorities in order to achieve that which serves the national interests. Shaykhs thus underline the advantages of working with the existing political regime and deemphasize the disadvantages, stressing the need to focus on *da'wa* work and the Islamization of society from below rather than from above.[32] They also argue that society ought to first have "the correct education" before challenging the political status quo with the aim of putting in place Islamic societies and states.

The implicit political stances taken by the Islamic groups mean that they helped to promote acquiescence to authority, at least in the short term, rather than democratic values and pluralist thinking. This had the net effect of both directly and indirectly reinforcing the political status of authoritarian rule, and was perhaps even more effective at doing so precisely because it is couched in apolitical terms that kept many Syrians from realizing its true political implications. Indeed, one of my interviewees noted that only by following the educational path prescribed by the Islamic groups could the violent contention that had surfaced in the Middle East region in the last few years be curbed:

> The regional and international environments are threatening, radical movements are emerging right and left, sometimes under the rubric of Islam, sometimes of Christianity, of secular ideologies, leftist movements, conservative currents...in Syria, there is...the realization that something has to be done. Call it [the renewal program of] spirituality, call it Islam, call it ideology, it is helpful and positive. Syrians are condemning violence, and condoning fairness (*'adel*) and forgiveness (*tasamuh*)...this sort of [Islamic] renewal is needed and much anticipated. Only intellectual renewal can stop radical thought and violent contention.

The priority given to the correct education also prompted many within Syria's Renewal Movement to argue that oppositionist Salafi Jihadists were a by-product of the crisis in religious education that existed, as well as the failure to adapt to the existing authoritarian political circumstances, something that true Muslims are required to do if they are to have any impact on their societies.[33] This is not only because jihadists advocated violent opposition to the state, but also because the Salafis tend to reject the shaykhs' traditional religious education and the institutional structures that undergird it, arguing that individuals are both able to teach themselves and to make their own decisions on Islam and

Islamic practices. The shaykhs of course experience this stance as threatening, and so hit back by promoting the traditional educational system as the correct path to be followed.

The politically accommodating yet simultaneously informed and aware rhetoric adopted by some of the most notable Syrian shaykhs in the last few years has granted the different Islamic groups the popular and official legitimacy needed to advance their discourse, their networks and their work. In particular, it is in explaining the strategic rationale behind the state's policies, in recognizing the state's shortcomings – albeit without being too judgmental – and in avoiding blindly justifying the state's actions that the movement has achieved so much popularity and thus success in promoting its "renewing" discourse.[34] One of my interviewee's statements sheds light on this last point:

> "certain Islamic shaykhs enjoy posing rhetorical questions and adding dramatic intonations, sometimes in admiration and other times in condemnation of the regime, depending on the group. Yet the ones who recognize the regime's shortcomings and successes are the most successful in Syria...Syrians are disillusioned with radical claims and promises of absolute truths." [author's translation]

This statement alludes to an important component in the discourse of the shaykhs, that is, its realistic and pragmatic approach. Indeed, most of the shaykhs have seemed satisfied with the status quo authoritarian political environment in Syria, and therefore did not appear to be seeking fundamental changes in existing political institutions.

The official Syrian Islamic message also promoted a moral-religious discourse that valorized co-habitation and bridging the supposed gaps between Syria's numerous religious cleavages. In a country where ethnic and religious diversity is ubiquitous, focusing on a universal interpretation of the faiths can be seen as an effective recruiting move. As a result of taking this stance, the state praises the role of Syria's Islamic *'ulama'* in maintaining national unity, enables their work, and opens up a space for them in the public sphere that non-Baathist secularist groups have not benefited from.

Yet notwithstanding the "tolerance of the other" and the accommodationist rhetoric of a majority of Syria's Islamic groups, the longer term implication of their rise is still a populace that is much more Islamized, and one might even argue that is also inadequately educated in the tenets of secularism, with its emphasis on civil liberties and political pluralism.[35] This in turn has important implications for when political change and, potentially, democratization come to Syria, in terms of how the populace would participate in the political process and what stances they would tend to take. At the same time, the Islamic groups' support for the exclusive authority of the political command, coupled with their own top-down authority structure that promotes an Islamic vision that tolerates but is not committed to compromise and constructive learning from and engagement with the other, also has important implications for how they would tend to participate in that political process.

Syria's Official Islam: Possible Categorizations
The majority of Syria's Islamic groups are politically quietist and small in size, the followings of shaykhs that tend to focus upon and have influence within their particular neighbourhood. But there are a number of Islamic groups that have a national presence and that have thus become some of the most prominent socio-political actors in the country.[36] Within the latter category, certain groups tend to advance a *moral* discourse in which Muslims and non-Muslims are characterized as sharing the same set of needs, goals and moral obligations. An example of such a group is the *Tajdeed* movement (see below). Other groups, such as al-Zayd movement, focus on the specifics of the *Islamic* aspect of their *da'wa*. Building upon this categorization, it is possible to organize Syria's revivalist movement into two broad groupings: 1) Those groups that promote a shared sense of human spirituality, primarily the Kuftariya Naqshbandiya order[37] and the *Tajdeed* (Renewal) movement led by Shaykh Muhammad Habash;[38] and, 2) those that focus upon the Islamic specificity of their *da'wa*, including the late 'Abd al-Karim al-Rifa'i's group (also known as the Zayd movement),[39] Sa'id al-Buti's "Middle Path" Islam,[40] Shaykh 'Abd al-Hadi al-Bani's *Jama'a*, Shaykh Khaznawi's group, and finally the originally secret "sisters" of Munira al-Qubaysi, which were officially recognized by the state in May 2006.

A different way of categorizing Syria's Islamic groups would be to distinguish those that were essentially pro-regime and that pay lip service to the political command from those that were simply apolitical, whether by their own choice or as a survival mechanism within the authoritarian context. The Zayd movement, the Qubaysis, and Shaykh al-Khaznawi's group fall into the latter bracket as groups that were "apolitical until further notice". Yet in so labelling them, it is simultaneously important to underline that they did not appear to be keen on spearheading a movement aimed at fundamental political change, though they might be expected to join in with such a movement once it was underway and clearly had momentum. This assertion is based upon interviews with some of their members, in which they articulated a sense that they were doing much better under the regime than they could expect to do in its absence. The primary reason for this is the lack of ideological alternatives that they have to compete with. Regarding the essentially pro-regime groups within the first category, they seem to be relatively integrated into the regime's network and thus supportive of its actions, a fact that makes it likely that they would have to reinvent their agenda and explain their previous commitments to the authoritarian regime in the case of regime change or democratization in the country.

While the groups were different in terms of their political stance relative to the regime, they all shared an interest in orienting their message towards Syrian youth. Some groups also succeeded at attracting the struggling lower classes – an example of the latter is the Zayd group, whose charity network is very widespread in the country. Reaching out to and connecting with this class is something that eluded the previous Islamic movement dominated by the Syrian Muslim Brothers. Indeed, the Brothers' discourse was more in favour of the traditional elite that was then on the decline, and it thus failed to galvanize more generalized public support.

The fact that some groups managed to connect with the struggling lower classes underlines the degree to which the Islamic movement had been re-invigorated and was growing ever more popular and influential, to the point that the regime began to re-examine its strategy towards the movement due to worries that the groups within it might become hard to keep in check.

Regime and Societal Reactions to the Increasing Influence of Islamic Groups

Signs of Fissures

As alluded to above, the regime's broad formula of controlled and selective re-invigoration of the Syrian Islamic movement has begun to show some cracks. In particular, the claim that only "moderate" and "pro-secular" – meaning pro-regime – Islamic groups and shaykhs were active and accommodated in Syria was undermined, for three main reasons:

1) The first had to do with the emergence of an outspoken and politically oriented group, *al-Tayar al-Islami al-Dimuqrati* (the Islamic Democratic Current).[41] This group surprised many when it issued a number of

statements in Syrian newspapers and on websites expressing its commitment to "democratic rule" and the need for political change, and denouncing the regime's corrupt and authoritarian ways.[42] More specifically, 2008 saw the Islamic Democratic Current calling on "the sons of the nation from all religions and ethnicities...our friends in faith, and our partners in the homeland" to unite in their support of the Islamic group. The message states, "we promise you citizenship and complete equality in rights and duties in return for your support of us in good times and in bad..."[43] [author's translation] The group's political ideas were summarized in a more recent statement published on a number of Syrian Websites that overtly attacked state officials and parliamentarians who conceal their animosity towards Islam within a discourse about secularism. The statement reads:

> The people have the right to choose their leaders and their representatives ...within a transparent and an honest parliamentary system...the enemies of Islam have shown their teeth, and some of them hide under the bitter disguise of secularism in order to uproot religion from society and life...holding up positions from within the regime in order to attack Islam...all with the knowledge and awareness of those within the Ministry of Endowment [Awqaf], the *ifta'* authorities and the National Assembly, who hold no real power...this minority of people attacks Islam...in the name of modernity, renewal, women's rights and Westernization [author's translation].[44]

Although the statement encourages the Islamic movement to continue to call for justice and democratic rule, its use of normative concepts such as "justice" and the "right path" without going into the details of what they theoretically and practically mean for the group could be interpreted as a potential red flag by members of the secular pro-democracy movement. For instance, do they mean a particularly Islamic understanding of justice, or a broader understanding that incorporates multiple viewpoints and that is predicated on dialogue? In the same vein is another statement by the group:

> "As for you, members of the Islamic Current, you are not a political party, though preaching for democracy and shura (consensus) is part of our call, you are not a welfare organization...and you are not a purpose-specific association meant to serve a narrow purpose. You are the beating heart of this nation, nurtured by the Quran...[author's translation]".

Also worth considering is this statement:

"As to you members of the Islamic Current, if asked about your call, say: we call to an all-encompassing Islam, pertinent to all sectors of life, and true to every place and time. The government is part of it, as freedom is part of its obligations. If told, this is part of the political; say, this is Islam as it should be, uncategorized." [author's translation].[45]

While these statements are potentially open to multiple interpretations, the Islamic Democratic Current has been much more definitive in denouncing Syria's official shaykhs for serving those in power rather than Islam.[46] Proof that the regime felt threatened by the group's attacks and its oppositional stance is the fact that its main leaders such as Yaser al-'Iti and Ahmad Tu'ma al-Khadr were imprisoned.

2) The second main reason stems from an August 2009 statement issued by elements within the Ba'th party that prompted outrage amongst a majority of the party's members.[47] The statement indicated that the state does not hold a "negative view" of the Islamic group led by Shaykh Hadi al-Bani, this despite the fact that the group promotes the creation of an Islamic political order in Syria and is considered by many to be one of the most radical Naqshbandi Islamic groups functioning inside the country. The statement caused the majority of Ba'thi members to declare that the Ba'th is no longer a party that upholds secularism and should be re-named "the Islamic Ba'th Party."[48] Some party members also demanded that the regime explain its compromises with and accommodation of a rising Islamic movement at the expense of the regime itself in the words of some.[49]

It is important to add here that the concerns regarding the movement's ideas were greatly increased by the fact that the regime had deliberately put a stop to any secular opposition or political discourse in Syria, thus emptying the country of alternative ideologies and movements that could provide a counterbalance to the Islamic sector. This could be interpreted as an effective use of divide and rule tactics, since Syrians have become polarized between those who support or at least tolerate the Islamic movement and those who either support secularism and are thus left with no alternative but to side with the regime as well as those who are against the Islamic movement and are also left with no alternative but to side with the regime. What will happen to this bifurcation of Syrians in the long term is of course difficult to predict.

3) The third reason for the view that not only "moderate" and pro-regime Islamic groups are active and being accommodated by the state is the leaking of controversial draft legislation in June 2009. This

legislation had been conceived as an amendment of the Personal Status Law. It caused a stir when it leaked since it showed that certain state officials lacked an affinity for the secular ideology of the Baath, and also gave rise to the suggestion that "radical Islamic elements" had assumed high-ranking positions within the Syrian political apparatus.

More particularly, the draft was interpreted as an attempt by Sunni radicals to strike a blow against demands from secularists for identical rights for men and women in Syria (as already stipulated in the Syrian Constitution) and as an attempt to generate a split between Sunnis and non-Sunni minorities in the country since it privileged a particularly Sunni religious vision in defining family law. According to pro-democracy critics, the draft legislation disregarded the concept of citizenship as articulated in the Syrian Constitution and consolidated the power of Islamic courts and other religious courts over all matters related to marriage, divorce and inheritance.[50] It also maintained so-called Islamic clauses that have been under attack by human rights lobbyists in the country since 1953. Other contentious clauses included continuing to allow polygamy for men, legalizing the marriage of children under the age of 18, requiring women to get their husbands' permission before being able to travel outside the country, and requiring women who have divorced and kept custody of the children to seek the approval of their husbands for what sort of work they do.

Generally speaking, the draft legislation ignored the recommendations of civil rights activists and committees. Indeed, even "moderate" interpretations of Islamic law endorsed by prominent Syrian shaykhs were not reflected in the draft legislation.[51] In Parliament, the speaker responded to the outcry by issuing a very brief statement to the effect that the leaked document was just a draft. And the legislation was not subsequently revisited by either the president or the Parliament. Yet the mere fact that it was drafted clearly proved startling to pro-democracy intellectuals, minority groups, Syrian women's groups and Ba'thi loyalists within the overall political apparatus. To focus on just one of these sub-groups' concerns, from the point of view of pro-democracy Syrians, what stood out was the drafters' disregard for international norms on human rights, minority rights and women's rights.

While some Syrians felt that the regime was to blame for the move away from secularism and its relative embrace of Islamic mores, others expressed their support for it as the only force able to protect Syrians from the radical Islamic threat. For its part, the regime refrained from commenting on the subject of the draft legislation, although it did subsequently take measures that could be interpreted as reining in the country's Islamic groups and cooling off its previous détente with them.

A Delicate Balance

The three events examined above underline the delicate balance that existed at the end of the 2000s between the Syrian Islamic sector and the regime, one in which statements and actions by one strongly risk affecting the other. They also show that the country's Islamic sector was far from unitary, with some groups continuing to play according to the rules set out by the regime and others attempting to circumvent or transcend them (as will be shown hereinafter). In general however, groups have tended to act at the expense of the country's historically secular public space. Indeed, for those within Syria's civil society who worry about the future of secularism within the country, there were plenty of reasons for concern: the number and popularity of Islamized spaces had increased exponentially; in the neighbourhoods around larger mosques shops had started to avoid playing music, some cafes stopped serving alcohol, women were harassed – mostly by other women – for not wearing the veil and people no longer ate outside during Ramadan; and, in 2006, large posters announcing the celebrations of *al-Mawled al-Nabawi* (the birth of the Prophet Muhammad) were prominent throughout the capital, something which Syrians had not seen for decades – in fact, those posters were so omnipresent that the Ba'thi posters celebrating the simultaneous annual national celebrations of Hafez al-Assad's "Corrective Movement" faded into the background.

One thing that is clear is that prominent figures within the Islamic movement such as shaykhs Salah Kuftaro and Sariya al-Rifa'i (as well as some of the latter's followers) had become more critical of the state, especially since Bashar's ascension to the presidency. For instance, Salah Kuftaro, who preaches to thousands of followers at the Abu al-Nur Mosque in Damascus and operates one of the largest Islamic charitable foundations in the country, called for an "Islamic democracy" in Syria, and pointed out the failings of secular Arab regimes in leading their countries.[52] Shaykhs within the Zayd movement also appeared to become more critical of the regime in their *khutbas*. Interestingly, whenever the shaykhs wished to criticize the political apparatus, they did so by attacking its secular aspect. And while these criticisms were still relatively low-key and unobtrusive, they were also becoming more daring than in previous years.

Furthermore, a number of religious groups have managed, in the last ten years, to acquire permits to open private schools and institutes all over the Syrian capital. They have done so by bribing officials and by exploiting administrative loopholes as well as their good relations with sympathetic officials within the Syrian bureaucracy. To give an example, al-Bawader school, which is now led by an Islamic group, was originally composed of ten classes and located in the old Mezzeh district of Damascus. Today, the Islamic group's successful investment projects and collection of money allowed the school to expand to as many as 40 classes and to relocate to the Kafer Suseh area. The religious groups also imposed their own curriculum and ensured that only carefully chosen teachers (usually affiliated with the Islamic group in control of the school) became part of their institution. In so doing, they managed to bypass the Syrian education ministry's controls and thus to avoid conforming to the ministry's regulations.

While accommodation and promotion of "moderate" or pro-regime Islam continued to be on the state's agenda, the increasing social and parliamentary weight of Islamic leaders and their allies became a source of concern to the regime. It is especially worried about the personalized and often informal nature of the network's activities – for instance, the fact that the Islamic network's shaykhs hold consultations with their followers in their private homes – which makes their work harder to monitor and control.[53] Indeed, one might wonder whether the regime is still in control of the piety movement. Relatedly, it is unclear how loyal co-opted groups are to the state despite the tightly knit relations that they forged with a number of state officials, and even to what degree the state and the Islamic groups are truly autonomous from one another. In regard to the latter issue, Islamic leaders have increasingly assumed high positions within the state and the government, to the point that the Ba´thist state almost seemed to be infiltrated and thus perhaps unsurprisingly divided on the issue of the "threat" posed by Islamic groups as well as more fundamentally over whether Syria's secular system ought to be maintained.

This push and pull over accommodating and incorporating the Islamic movement has prompted outrage amongst pro-regime secularists, who argued that the country's loss of its secular ethos would lead to political and social instability. It also outraged pro-democracy secularists, who claimed that the Islamic movement was reinforcing the authoritarian political culture within the country. Both groups agreed that Syrians have many ideological, religious and ethnic affinities and should not feel under attack by the Sunni piety movement. But they were divided over what the state should do, with pro-regime secularists endorsing the use of an iron fist that would deal with any dissenting movement once and for all, while pro-democracy intellectuals wanted to see true democratization taking place within the country.

As to the political leadership, its concerns did not result in a clear clampdown in the manner of the suppression of the political liberalization known as the "Damascus Spring" (which was initiated only a couple of weeks after Bashar's rise to power in 2000). Nonetheless, the accommodation of the Islamic movement became more nuanced and was even curtailed after 2005, particularly due to fears surrounding the possibility of a rapprochement between the secular Syrian opposition, Syrian Islamists abroad, and some members of the domestic Islamic groups.[54] For instance, in 2005, the Jamal al-Atasi civil society forum was closed down and its administrator, Hussein al-'Odat, was arrested for having read to the attendees of the forum a statement on behalf of the Syrian Muslim Brotherhood. Thus the forum, which had earlier survived the repressive measures undertaken by the state against civil society following the "Damascus Spring," had apparently pushed too far. The message sent was that only certain groups would be allowed to be a part of the Syrian Islamic movement, and that a political Islamic group like the Muslim Brothers would not be tolerated.

In May 2005, prominent Islamic leader Muhammad al-Khaznawi was found dead under suspicious circumstances. While the Syrian state said that the shaykh was a moderate leader and an ally of the state - after all, he was the second in command at Damascus' *Ma'had al-Da'wa al-Islamiya* (The Institute of Islamic Da'wa) – his followers argued that his assassination followed particularly vociferous sermons denouncing the Syrian government, which had in turn caused him to be targeted by the regime. Indeed, the shaykh was described as a powerful critic of the regime, particularly because of his great charisma and the resultant influence that he exercised over those who attended his Islamic institute, where he taught the Quran and Islamic jurisprudence. Since this institute was based in the northern Syrian city of Qamishli, which is predominantly inhabited by Kurds, some reports have claimed that Shaykh Khaznawi represented the Islamic Kurdish political opposition in Syria and that he was interested in aligning the Syrian Kurds' struggle against the regime with that of the Muslim Brotherhood, an aim that led him to meet with leaders from the Muslim Brotherhood in February of 2005 in Brussels, Belgium.[55] Thus while Syrian officials blamed his mysterious death on radical Islamists who opposed his reformist and inclusive interpretation of Islam, the Shaykh's family and followers remain convinced that the Syrian secret service assassinated him. After his death, tensions in the city of al-Qamishli were very high, resulting in instances of civil disobedience that caused the death of one police officer and the wounding of a dozen protesters.[56]

March 2006 saw the regime move to outlaw political contacts and the forging of alliances with any foreign element or government.[57] This move was due to its fear of an Islamist upsurge taking advantage of the opportunity presented by the country's burgeoning domestic civil society (both secular and Islamic). As Eyal Zisser writes: "This fear of a fundamentalist wave that threatened to sweep over the country had many partners, even outside the ranks of the regime, which could explain their support for it or more precisely their reservations about the activities of the reformist camp."[58]

The month before, in February 2006, a new opposition coalition emerged that united former Vice President 'Abdu Halim Khaddam and the Syrian Muslim Brotherhood under the name of the National Salvation Front.[59] The state responded to this challenge by, again, sending a clear message. On the 28th of February 2006, the director of the Damascus *Waqf* (religious endowments), Muhammad Khaled al-Mu'tem, issued a decree that banned religious lessons from Syria's mosques, with Quranic lessons reduced to once or twice a week rather than being given on a daily basis. Furthermore, the mosques and *zawiyas* [Sufi prayer rooms] were told to close their doors in between prayers unless they received a special permit from the Ministry of Endowments. Most importantly, the decree also banned mosques and *zawiyas* from receiving any donations without reporting them first to the Ministry of Endowments. It was only following a massive mobilization of the religious elite that parts of the ban were lifted, with the influential Member of Parliament Muhammad Habash intervening to resolve the situation.[60]

Although hundreds of Islamist prisoners had been released in since 2000, many Syrians were also detained during the same period. Indeed, the Syrian security court handed down prison sentences to dozens of alleged Islamists accused of belonging to radical Islamic groups and of planning "unlawful" activities in Syria.[61] This crackdown continued in early 2010, when the state again outlawed Hadi al-Bani's Islamic group. In June of that year, Islamists allegedly belonging to a group plotting against the state were caught and imprisoned. And that same month, the state banned the *niqab* in the country's educational institutions in a move that was timed to coincide with France's ban on the wearing of the facial covering. As a result, teachers who refused to stop wearing the *niqab* were removed from their posts and placed in administrative positions. The logic behind this decision was that Syria needed to hold on to its secular heritage and culture and more importantly that this sort of "radical" attire sends the wrong message to Syrian children, whether about women, Islam or Syria.[62]

These latest events spurred a series of fissiparous community reactions that coalesced into three distinct points of view. The first wanted the authoritarian regime to take control of the situation and put an end to the Islamic movement that had got beyond its control, regardless of the consequences. The second blamed the policies of the authoritarian regime for facilitating the rise of Islamic groups in a country long known for its secular heritage and believed that fundamentalist and sectarian ideologies had been catered to by a regime looking to divide Syrian society in order to continue to rule the country. Those holding this point of view wanted to derail Syria's Islamic renewal by strengthening the secular pro-democracy movement. It is important to note here that the Syrian Muslim Brothers can be considered part of this school of thought since the Brotherhood's leadership had expressed its commitment to a secular and democratic Syria. And finally, a third group saw the Islamic movement as the only centre of power that could bring about regime change, thus either supporting the movement's program or believing that an Islamic Uprising was better than the status quo. Those in favour of democracy within this group argue that an Islamic uprising would eventually lead to democratic change.

Conclusion

The success of the various Syrian Islamic groups at operating in the space available to them to propagate a comprehensive Islamic sphere that is attracting a growing membership in an otherwise secular public space, showed them to be masters at the game of *realpolitik*. Not only did they efficiently adapt to the authoritarian context of Syrian politics, they also made themselves indispensable to a political elite that was widely seen as illegitimate and that had thus sought to forge coalitions with powerful societal forces. At first glance, the content of the Islamic discourse being propagated seemed to be fairly traditional, focusing on a variety of typical themes that resonate with their supporters.[63] At the same time, though, the aims and scope of this literature are different from those of the previous Islamic movement in Syria, notably the Muslim Brotherhood. In particular, the new groups shifted their focus from politics to ethical philosophy and political quietism. The movement now aimed to elevate society's Islamic ethos and the sense of duty that individuals feel towards the other members of their community, while its literature's focus was Islamic change from below through renewal.

This shift allowed the Syrian Islamic movement to survive and even prosper under the Baath, effectively becoming an integral and influential part of the socio-political establishment. Indeed, the resurgence of a powerful and diverse Islamic network in the country prompted President Bashar al-Assad to call for a new relationship with Islamic groups in Syria. Many observers saw such a compromise as having been forced upon the president because the religious bourgeoisie was now considered to be an important client of the regime, as well as because of concerns about spill over effects of the political instability in Iraq and the emergence of militant Islamist activity in the region. This paper has argued that the rising influence of these Islamic groups stems from the conscious support of a regime that wanted to repress the secular and the Islamic political opposition. It thus persecuted the secularists and the anti-regime Islamists to the point that they could no longer function within the country's authoritarian environment while striking a deal with the non-political Islamic movement that allowed them to operate in Syria as long as they remained politically quietist.

Yet in spite of this relatively long-standing rapprochement between the regime and the Syrian shaykhs, the former began to have strong concerns regarding the Islamic groups' willingness to continue playing the game according to the agreed rules, and started to wonder whether some would move to the forefront of opposition activism if circumstances permitted. These concerns go some way toward explaining the Syrian state's repealing of a number of its accommodations of the Islamic sector over the five years 2005-2010. Such shifts show that Bashar al-Assad seemed to be following in his father's footsteps by using comparable domestic socio-political manipulations in the face of existential threats similar to the ones faced by his father at the beginning of his rule, which included economic malaise within the country, instability in the region, and a legitimacy crisis for the regime. A further complicating factor was that Syria's Islamic groups were far from being homogeneous, which necessitated targeted actions aimed at particular groups such as al-Tayar al-Islami, with other shaykhs being given more organizational space.

The regime coalition itself appeared to be divided between those who were advocating accommodation and those who pushed for containment. Whether these mixed signals were actually the result of a split within the ruling group or are merely evidence of a carrot and stick strategy, one thing is clear: the state's attempts to allow the "moderate" groups – meaning those that are pro-regime – to exist while simultaneously controlling the "radical" groups – meaning those that are anti-regime – had become increasingly fraught.

The pro-democracy opposition was also divided. Some believe that any change is better than a continuation of the status quo while others are afraid that the Islamization of society at the expense of other groups will only lead to more authoritarianism. Regardless, it was clear even in 2010, that Syria was heading towards more instability. And within that increasingly unstable environment, there were a multitude of questions related to the Islamic sector and the place of Islam within Syrian society that were becoming ever more pressing. In the words of one interviewee:

> "How can we rate these groups? First of all, what is radical and what is not? Plus, some of these groups are radical on certain issues but rather accommodating on others. Is wanting people not to eat outside their homes during the fasting hours of Ramadan a radical expectation in general? Does it predict a radical political attitude later on? How about scaring girls into veiling [by mentioning the fires of hell]? [What about] saying that the role of women is to raise children and stay at home?"

What is clear in these questions is that many Syrians were still grappling with the repercussions arising from the shifts in the socio-political environment that had vaulted the groups that make up the Islamic sector into the ranks of the nation's most important actors. What is less clear is how to answer them in a manner that is satisfactory to all Syrians. Yet at the same time, they are too important to ignore or to simply put off – thus it seems likely that the Syrian soul searching regarding the proper balance between secularism and public religiosity will continue for the foreseeable future.

---

[1] This paper was written in late 2010 and frames the Islamic context in the country up to that year. I am indebted in the writing of this paper to Robert Stewart, who has always taken the time to patiently read, edit, and comment upon my work.

[2] Religious revival does not necessarily mean an increase in religiosity, rather it refers to an increase in *overt*, public religious observance and thus of a reassertion of one's religious practice within the public sphere. *Islamic* revival refers to the permeation of society with activities, organizations, speech, and attire that are considered to be "Islamic", and that palpably impact the way of life of Syrians on a daily basis. The emphasis here on the Islamic revival should not be construed as meaning that there is not also a Christian revival in Syria; but discussion of this topic is beyond the scope of this paper.

[3] The political ambitions of some within the Syrian Muslim Brethren have tended to overshadow the apolitical activities of the rest of Syria's Islamic

groups such as the Naqshbanidiya, the Shadhiliya and the Rifa'iya, among others. See: Line Khatib, *Islamic Revivalism in Syria: the Rise and Fall of Bathist Secularism*, (New York and London: Routledge, 2011); *al-Hayat*, 18 June 2005; and the Syrian Ministry of *Awqaf*, studies and statistics 31.12. 2007 and 31.12.2008. To name a few of the works by the expanding scholarship on Syria's apolitical Islamic organizations and their leaders' dogma: Annabelle Böttcher, "Islamic Teaching Among Sunni Women in Syria," in Bowen and Early, ed., *Everyday Life in the Muslim Middle East*, 2002; Idem, *Official Sunni and Shi'i Islam in Syria*, (San Domenic: European University Institute, 2002); Andreas Christmann, "'The Form is Permanent, but the Content Moves': The Qur'anic Text and its Interpretation(s) in Mohamad Shahrour's *Al-Kitab wa l-Quran*," *Die Welt des Islam*, 43, 2003: 143-172; idem, "73 Proofs of Dilettantism: The Construction of Norm and Deviancy in the Responses to 'al-Kitab wa'l-Qur'an: Qira'a Mu'asira' by Mohamad Shahrour," *Die Welt des Islam*, 45, 2005: 20-73; Leif, Stenberg, "Naqshbandiyya in Damascus: Strategies to Establish and Strengthen the Order in a Changing Society," in Elisabeth Özdalga, ed., *Naqshbandis in Western and Central Asia - Change and Continuity*, (Istanbul: Swedish Research Institute in Istanbul, 1999), pp. 101-116; idem, "Young, Male and Sufi Muslim in the City of Damascus," in Jørgen Bæck Simonsen, ed., *Youth and Youth Culture in the Contemporary Middle East*, (Aarhus: Aarhus University Press, 2005), pp. 68-91; Thomas Pierret and Kjetil Selvik, "Limits of Authoritarian Upgrading in Syria: Private Welfare, Islamic Charities, and the Rise of the Zayd Movement," *International Journal of Middle Eastern Studies*, 41 (2009): 595-614.

[4] See for instance, Mustafa al-Siba'i, *Asdaq al-Itijahat al-Fikriya fi al-sharq al-Arabi* [The Sincerest Intellectual Directions in the Arab East], (Damascus: Dar al-Waraq, 1998); idem, *Islamuna* [Our Islam], (Damascus: Dar al-Waraq, 2001); Muhammad Sa'id Ramadan al-Buti, *Kalimat fi Munasabat* (Words on Occasions), (Damascus: Dar al-Fikr, 2002); Muhammad Umar al-Haji, *'Alamiyat al-Da'wa ila allah ta'ala* [The Global Call to God], (Damascus: Dar al-Maktabi, 2007); Muhammad Ratib al-Nabusli, *Muqawimat al-Taklif*, (Damascus: Dar al-Maktabi, 2005).

[5] See Weismann, "Sa'id Hawwa and Islamic Revivalism in Ba'thist Syria," *Middle Eastern Studies*, 29 October 1993, pp. 144-146.

[6] It is important to note that a national version of secularism (based on the French model) has been part of Syria's political and intellectual heritage since the early 20th century. Ba'thist secularism was once seen as verging on atheism - indeed, in the 1960s, Syria's Islamic movement considered the Ba'th discourse to be atheistic, and accused the party of corrupting the public with their message. In the late 1970s, Saudi King Faysal and Egyptian President Anwar Sadat went so far as to call it an "evil" Party. See Robert W. Olson, *The B'ath and Syria*, (Princeton, N.J.: The Kingston Press, Inc., 1982), p. 122; Nikolaos Van Dam, *The Struggle for Power in Syria*, (London & New York: I.B. Tauris Publishers, 1996), p.93.

[7] Syria's secular cultural heritage is closer to the French system of *laïcité* rather than to Anglo-Saxon secularism. As such, it perceives the public space as closed off to religion, something which the Ba'th regime had actively pursued in the 1960s. The last 20 years have seen the country oscillate towards secularism

and away from *laïcité*, in other words, from a secularism which is essentially against faith to one that sees itself existing with faith. For an interesting work on the difference between *laïcité* and secularism in confronting Islam, see Olivier Roy, *Secularism Confronts Islam*, (New York: Columbia University Press, 2007). In one recent article, a Syrian intellectual dubbed Syrian secularism "*Ilmaniya Mashriqiya fi Dimashq*" [Levantine secularism in Damascus], see *al-Hayat*, 22 June 2007.

[8] Syria is an ideologically, ethnically and religiously diverse society. In terms of ethnicities, the country is 90.3% Arab, 9.7% Kurdish, Armenian, and other. In terms of religion, 74% of Syrians are Sunni Muslim, 16% are other Muslim (including Alawite and Druze), and 10% are Christian (various denominations). The country also includes small Jewish communities in Damascus, Al Qamishli and Aleppo. See the Syrian Central Bureau of Statistics, 2009 and Syrian Statistical Abstract at http://wwwcbssyr.org; the CIA World Factbook at http:// www.cia.gov/cia/publications/factbook/goes/sy.html

[9] Elaph website at http//:www.elaph.com (28 June 2010) (Last viewed 30 June 2010).

[10] See al-Jazeera TV, 18 July 2010. This was, however, reversed in 2011.

[11] It was clearly stated during the Ba'th Party conference of June 2005 that banning Islamic groups from expressing themselves could potentially lead to their radicalization, especially given the regional context and the war in neighbouring Iraq.

[12] Khatib, *Islamic Revivalism in Syria*, p. 50.

[13] *Ibid.*, Part II.

[14] *Ibid.*, chapter 7.

[15] *Ibid.*, p. 106.

[16] "Officially" because one might say that, practically speaking, Bashar al-Asad has only continued his father's policies of accommodation and cooptation. See Khatib, *Islamic Revivalism in Syria*.

[17] Eyal Zisser, "Syria, the Ba'th Regime and the Islamic Movement: Stepping on a New Path?" *The Muslim World* 95 (January 2005). Khatib, *Islamic Revivalism in Syria*, chapter 6.

[18] See for instance the Syrian President's meeting with the Turkish minister of religious affairs on 23 April, 2010.

[19] See *al-Hayat*, 05 April 2006; *al-Safir*, 06 April 2006.

[20] Zisser, "Syria, the Ba'th Regime and the Islamic Movement: Stepping on a New Path?" p. 43; idem, *Commanding Syria: Bashar al-Asad and the First Years in Power*, (New York: I.B.Tauris, 2007), p. 93.

[21] Shortly after his 1982 decree forbidding the wearing of headscarves, Hafez al-Asad reversed his initial stance (although the decree itself was not revoked) and affirmed less than a year later in one of his rare presidential addresses that: "In Syria, dress is a matter of private and personal choice...customs and traditions cannot be overcome by violence." Oral sources; quoted in Annika Rabo, "Gender, State and Civil Society," Hann, Chris and Elizabeth Dunn, *Civil Society: Challenging Western Models*, (London & New York: Routledge, 1996), p. 170. In one conversation I had with a school director, whose institution received clear orders in the early 1980s to forbid

veiling in the school, she admitted to having been shocked and confused by the speech.

[22] Syrian Human Rights Committee at www.shrc.org/data/aspx/d6/586.aspx (last viewed November 2010).

[23] Zisser, "Syria, the Ba'th Regime and the Islamic Movement: Stepping on a New Path?"; Joshua Landis, "The Syrian Opposition," *Washington Quarterly* 30, 1 (Winter 2006-2007), p. 47.

[24] *Al-Hayat*, 29 March 2006; Cham Press available at: Http://www.champress.net (30 March 2006).

[25] Moubayed, "Islamic Revival in Syria," (Online). See also *The New York Times*, 6 April 2006.

[26] Pierret/Selvik, "Limits of "Authoritarian Upgrading" in Syria", pp. 600-601.

[27] See Khatib, *Islamic Revivalism in Syria*, chapter 5.

[28] See for instance al-Buti, *al-Ta'aruf 'ala al-Dhat Huwa al-Tariq ila al-Islam* [Knowing the Self is the way to Islam], (Damascus: Dar al-Fikr, n.d.) See also Muhammad 'Abd al-Satar, "Al-Tajdid fi al-Fikr al-Islami," delivered on 7 March, 2009. Available at http://www.syrianawkaf.org.

[29] According to *Syria Today*, October 2008, publishers of religious texts are finding a highly receptive audience, allowing them to expand their distribution networks and thus to attract more readers, which has lead to a doubling in sales over the last few years: "It's an economic fact that religious books are at the heart of publishing in Syria," said 'Adnan Salem, owner of Syria's largest religious publishing house *al-Fikr* (The Thought), which has branches in a number of Arab countries, including Algeria, Yemen, Egypt and the Gulf States.

[30] This sort of emphasis underlines Olivier Roy's argument that these modern groups have turned fundamentalist and neo-fundamentalist rather than into Islamist groups. See Olivier Roy, *The Failure of Political Islam*, (Cambridge: Harvard University Press, 1996).

[31] The state's vision of Islam is available on two main websites: the Syrian Ministry of Awqaf and the Syrian Ministry of Culture. For a prominent shaykh's understanding of the Syrian state, see Muhammad Shahrur, *Tajfif Manabi'al-Irhab*, (Damascus: al-Ahali, 2008), pp. 140-141.

[32] See section on the Kuftariya order below; also lecture delivered at the Asad Library in Damascus by Shaykh Muhammad 'Abd al-Satar, "Al-'Alaqat al-Insaniya fi al-Islam." Available at http://www.Syrianawkaf.org.

[33] See Khatib, *Islamic Revivalism in Syria*, pp. 150-153. See also Shahrur, *Tajfif Manabi'al-Irhab*, p.21, and pp. 239-241. Also, observation based on recordings of weekly lessons delivered by prominent shaykhs such as Abd al-Fatah al-Buzum, Usama al-Rifa'i, and Tawfiq Ramadan, under the tutelage of the Ministry of Awqaf at the Umayad mosque, addressing *Fiqh*, *Hadith* and *Usul al-Fiqh* and *al-'Ibadat*.

[34] It is important to note that the Syrian Islamic discourse is nuanced, complex and sometimes ambiguous, depending on the group studied, but also on the shaykh or shaykha being examined within a particular group. Therefore, it is important to stress that the points presented above are general ones, meant to form a basis for the study of Syria's "official" or "legal" Islamic movement.

[35] *Nahj al-Islam*, the Ministry of Endowments' official Islamic magazine, often features the words of President Bashar al-Asad on the first page. Generally speaking, the magazine focuses on addressing the state's concerns as regards issues such as the meaning of tolerance, co-habitation and radicalism, whether under the rubrics of literature, evolutionary theory, law or the economy. The writers do so by interpreting references to the Quran, the Hadith and the Sunna. The journal tends to emphasize the need for Islamic knowledge and Islamic integration within the socio-political structure, in order to wage a successful struggle against macro and micro-level ills. Significantly, *Nahj al-Islam* has lately begun to take on a more authoritative tone, thus possibly providing a hint into the Islamic movement's increasing prominence.

[36] Personal interviews in Damascus, April 2008. There are at least 20 active Islamic groups in Syria at the time of this writing, which include Ahmad Hassoun's Institute in Aleppo and Shaykh Mashouq Khaznawi's in Qamishli.

[37] The Kuftariya Naqshbandiya encompasses prominent shaykhs such as the late Ahmad Kuftaro, Shaykh Salah Kuftaro and Shaykha Wafa' Kuftaro. The most prominent order in Syria is the Naqshbandiya. Other prominent orders are the Shadhiliya, and the Rifa'iya. Most groups in Syria do not follow a rigid Naqshbandi way, though they are impacted by it. For instance, Ahmad Habash, Munira al-Qubaysi and Abd al-Karim al-Rafi'i are of the Kuftariya Naqshabandi school. The Shadhiliya order includes the teachings of Shaykhs 'Abd al-Rahman al-Shaghuri, Shukri al-Luhafi, Shaykh Saleh al-Hamawi, and Muhammad Hisham al-Burhani. Their *Zikr* sessions are held at the Nuriya Mosque, al-Sadat Mosque, and al-Tawba Mosque in Damascus. The Rifa'iya order includes the teaching of Ahmad al-Habbal at the Mosque of Badr al-Din in Damascus.

[38] Dr. Habash has published dozens of books and papers in Arabic. For an introductory article with Dr. Habash discussing his revivalist movement, see *Asharq Al-Awsat*, 3 February 2006. For Western works, see Paul L. Heck, "Religious Renewal in Syria: the Case of Muhammad al-Habash," *Islam and Christian-Muslim Relations*, 15, 2004: 185-207; idem, "Muhammad al-Habach et le dialogue interreligieux," in Baudouin Dupret (ed.), *La Syrie au Présent*, (Paris: Sinbad / Actes Sud, 2007).

On his sister Shaykha Huda Habash, see Hilary Kalmbach, "Social and Religious Change in Damascus: One Case of Female Religious Authority," *British Journal of Middle Eastern Studies*, 35, 2008: 37-57.

[39] 'Abd al-Karim al-Rifa'i's *da'wa* team includes shaykhs such as Sariya al-Rifa'i, Usama al-Rifa'i, Na'im Íriksusa and Nadhir al-Maktabi, among others.

[40] See Christmann, "Ascetic Passivity in Times of Extreme Activism: the Theme of Seclusion in a Biography by al-Buti," in Philip S. Alexander et al. eds., *Studia Semitica: the Journal of Semitic Studies Jubilee Volume*, (Oxford: Oxford University Press, 2005), 279-303. See also, Fred de Jong, "Les confréries mystiques musulmanes au Machreq arabe," in Alexandre Popovic and Gilles Veinstein, eds., *Les Ordres mystiques dans l'Islam: Cheminements et situation actuelle* (Paris: Editions de l'EHESS, 1986).

⁴¹ Some observers claim that the group is believed to be an off-shoot of the Syrian Muslim Brotherhood, composed of the group's remaining loyalists inside the country.
⁴² Private communication. See also Kuluna Shuraka' website at http://all4syria.info/content/view/140/65/ (12-08-2009).
⁴³ See al-Marfa' at http:www.almarfaa.net/?p=243 (7 September 2008).
⁴⁴ Statement published on Kuluna Shuraka' website at: http://all4syria.info/content/view/13055/39/ (23-08-2009). For more on al-Tayar, see Kahtib, *Islamic Revivalism in Syria,* pp. 177-180.
⁴⁵ See Kuluna Shuraka' at: http://all4syria.info/content/view/13055/39/ (23 August 2009).
⁴⁶ Alluding to shaykhs such as Muhammad Habash and Ahmad Hassoun. For more on these, see: Khatib, *Islamic Revivalism in Syria,* chapter 7.
⁴⁷ Akhbar al-Sharq website at http://www.thelevantnews.net (10 November 2009).
⁴⁸ See All for Syria at: http://all4syria.info/content/view/16751/96/ (Last visited 12 November, 2009).
⁴⁹ Stated by Akhbar al-Sahrq at http://www.levantnews.net (10 November 2009).
⁵⁰ For a brief overview of the draft and reactions to it, see Syria Briefing, IWPR Report, 12 June 2009; *Gulf News,* 23 June 2009.
⁵¹ For instance, in his Islamic *Tajdeed* (Renewal) program, Shaykh Muhammad Habash asserts the right of the woman to state the conditions of her marriage in her marriage contract. He rejects the marriage of children under the age of 18, and states that women have the right to divorce their husbands with or without the man's approval. The *Tajdeed* program (pp. 18-20).
⁵² Moubayed, "Islamic Revival in Syria." See also *The Washington Post,* 23 January 2005; and *The Daily Star,* 18 January 2005; See also Salah Kuftaro, "Al-Wihda al-Islamiya wa Tahadiyat al-'Asr," *Nahj al-Islam,* 1 May 2009. Salah Kuftaro is now serving a prison sentence for "embezzlement".
⁵³ According to Ibrahim Hamidi (*al-Hayat* newspaper), licensing the Qubaysi Sisters to operate openly and within Syrian mosques was a way to monitor their activity. See *al-Hayat,* 3 May 2006.
⁵⁴ Zisser, *Commanding Syria,* pp. 86-91. The action was directed at the entire civil society movement, but touched mainly the secular opposition: the regime struck back by using emergency powers and restrictive legislation such as the 1958 Law on Associations and Private Societies (Law No. 93) to control civil society groups' access and ties to the Syrian community, and to prohibit them from operating as legally-recognized groups. The regime also struck back by harassing and arresting a number of the movement's intellectuals, by denying requests by political forums to have their permits renewed, and by waging a war against the dissidents in the media. "Under the provisions of Law No. 93, the Syrian Ministry of Social Affairs and Labor (MoSAL) controls the registration of all civil society associations and has wide jurisdiction to intervene in the internal governance and day-to-day operations of any association. Associations must notify MoSAL of their meetings, and representatives of the ministry have the right to attend. In addition, MoSAL has the authority to regulate the ties of any local group with the international community, ensuring that local

associations are severely restricted in their ability to finance their operations or seek advice, expertise, support, and cooperation from abroad." See: http://makkah.wordpress.com/2007/10/31/strangling-human-rights-in-syria/ (Last viewed 10 June 2008).

[55] See al-Khaznawi website at http://www.khaznawi.de/khaznawi/2005/3.htm; see also *New York Times*, 2 July 2005.

[56] *Ibid.*

[57] Joshua Landis and Joe Pace, "The Syrian Opposition," *The Washington Quarterly*, 30, 1, Winter 2006-2007, p. 60.

[58] Eyal Zisser, *Commanding Syria: Bashar al-Asad and the First Years in Power,"* p. 93.

[59] As noted earlier, this coalition ceased to exist in May 2009.

[60] *Al-Hayat*, 29 March 2006; See also *As-safir*, 6 April 2006. For commentaries on the issue ranging from the secularists to the religious, see http://www.champress.com (March 30, 2006). See also "Syria Rescinds Ban on Religious Lessons in Mosques" (http://faculty-staff.ou.edu/L/Joshua.M.Landis-1/syriablog/index.html, 30 March 2006).

[61] See the Syrian Human Rights Committee at http: //www.shrc.org (see for instance 29 July 2010).

[62] *Al-Watan* newspaper (Syria), 30 June 2010 (This ban was repealed in 2011, during the Syrian uprising).

[63] The discourse refers to the Quran and the Hadith, relating stories from the life of the Prophet and his companions, thus explaining Islamic precepts, the religious duties of Muslims, the fundamental methods of *Ijtihad* according to *Shari'a* (Islamic Law), and the ways to entice good and forbid evil, to name a few.

3
The Discourses of the Damascene Sunni 'Ulama during the 2011 Revolution[1]

Jawad Qureshi

The Arab Spring and Religion

The events that sparked the Arab Spring date back to December 2010 and occurred in the Tunisian city of Sidi Bouzid, where Muhamed Bouazizi, a street vendor who could not afford to pay the bribes needed for a permit, immolated himself after being harassed by the local police. Protests and rallies took off throughout Tunisia and led to the unexpected ousting of President Zine El Abidine Ben Ali in January 2011. Shortly thereafter, a wave of protests swept across the Middle East that resulted in the resignations of both Egyptian president Hosni Mubarak and Yemeni president Ali Abdullah Saleh and the killing of Libyan leader Muammar Qaddafi. Of the countries that saw mass protests, only two regimes have so far resisted being toppled, the monarchy of King Hamad al-Khalifa of Bahrain and the Syrian Baath Party under Bashar al-Assad. More than a year since the beginning of these events, the monarchy in Bahrain has successfully quelled the uprising while in Syria the Baath regime remains engaged in fighting an emboldened populace that does not appear ready to give up.

Over the past year, the role of religion and religious actors has been a recurring concern for many observers. At the start of the Arab Spring, analysts were keen to note that the Tunisian and Egyptian revolutions were not led by Islamists and that there was a general absence of religion and ideology in the rhetoric of the protesters. In Egypt, the conspicuous absence of Al-Azhar's leadership from the demonstrations was made up for by images of Azharis—recognizable by their distinct white turban and red tarboush—standing alongside protesters, including also Coptic Christians, re-assuring many that sectarian fears and identity politics could be put aside in order to deal with the more fundamental problems posed by the thirty years of the Mubarak regime. Even Shaykh Yusuf al-Qaradawi, the famous Egyptian religious scholar based in Qatar, in his Friday sermon on February 18th in Tahrir Square, was congratulatory to the Egyptian revolutionaries for their display of national unity across religious lines. After the revolutions, religion remains an issue of concern. While theocracies and "the Iranian model" of *wilāyat al-faqīh* (the guardianship of the jurist) seem to be in little favour, the focus of observers seems to centre on the role of religion in shaping policy and law, and "the Turkish model" of Islamism has greater currency while the fear of Salafism looms large. This concern is certainly justified, particularly after the victory of the Islamist al-Nahda Party in Tunisian elections, the strong showing at the polls in Egypt's elections of the Salafi al-Nur party and the Muslim Brotherhood's Freedom and Justice Party, as well as the religious character of many of Libya's revolutionary fighters.

At the time of writing, protests and government crackdowns continue throughout Syria, where men of religion and their institutions have played a prominent role in shaping both sides of the protests since they began. In an authoritarian regime such as Syria's, where political gatherings are banned, Friday prayers are the only occasion when people can legally gather en-masse. There are two consequences of this. The first is that in a fairly religiously observant society such as Syria's, 'ulama have been uniquely situated in being able to address large public gatherings in a manner that other actors in society cannot. Secondly, mosques have been the primary sites from which protests are launched and also the targets of government crackdowns. Each Friday thus presented an opportunity for the 'ulama to intervene in events. Also, as the government crackdown became increasingly violent and greater numbers of protestors were killed, the funeral prayers held at mosques re-inscribed the mosque as a site of opposition. Funeral processions carrying the bier of Friday's dead to the graveyard often turned into protests, drawing further government repression. In this way, particularly in the beginning of the Syrian Uprising, mosques served as important sites for resistance and violence.

This paper presents a narrative of events in Damascus as protests emerged from the last week of March to May 2011, focusing on the public interventions of Sunni 'ulama as events progressed.[2] Throughout this narrative, I pay attention to how the 'ulama in question position themselves with respect to both the government and the protestors, concentrating on their modes of reasoning. Rather than categorizing the positions taken by the 'ulama under general frameworks, I have chosen to provide a linear narrative to convey a sense of the progression and escalation of events. The materials analyzed include sermons, public lessons and eulogies at funerals in addition to appearances on state and satellite television.[3] I focus on Damascus because, in addition to being the seat of power, it is difficult to gather and verify information from the cities and towns where protests and government crackdowns have been most marked–Daraa, Latakia, Douma, Banyas, Jisr Shughour, Hama and Homs. Also, the author was present in Damascus between March and April 2011 and witnessed a number of the events mentioned below first-hand. Some of the incidents not witnessed directly were verified shortly after their occurrence through interviews with eyewitnesses.

March, 2011: The Start of the Syrian Uprising

As protests were spreading throughout the Arab world in January and February 2011, a series of isolated events took place in Syria that unsuccessfully tried to spark the fire of revolution. These included the self-immolation of a man in Hasaka à la Bouazizi, a "Day of Rage" in Damascus on February 4-5, a protest in the Hariqa Souq in Damascus on February 17 after the son of a shop owner was hit by a policeman, protests in Damascus' Marjeh Square on March 16th and an anti-Qaddafi rally in front of the Libyan embassy on March 22nd (at which over one hundred people were arrested). Each of these was put down relatively quickly and failed to inspire a mass uprising.

On March 6th in the southern city of Daraa, fifteen boys aged 10 to 15 were arrested for writing anti-government graffiti on the wall of their school, including the slogan of the Arab Spring, "The people want to bring down the government" (*al-sha'b yurīd isqāṭ al-niẓām*). Family members of the boys pleaded for their release with local authorities to no avail. On March 18th, several thousand protestors marched from the al-'Umari mosque after Friday prayers demanding the release of the boys as well as greater political freedoms. The government met the protestors with riot police, water cannons, tear gas and, eventually, live ammunition. Four protestors were killed that day and dozens more were injured. Throughout Syria, small protests flared up after Friday prayers, including the Ummawi Mosque in Damascus. Throughout the week of March 19-24, both the protests and the government crackdown in Daraa increased proportionately, with the former growing in numbers and the latter in violence. A circle of violence was created: each protest was met with a heavy hand from the government, resulting in more funerals, whose processions became protests, which were met with more violence and death. News from Daraa spread throughout the country primarily via satellite channels, in particular al-Jazeera and BBC Arabic. Throughout the day, they aired gritty images captured on cell phone cameras accompanied by voice-overs from analysts still jubilant about events in Tunis and Egypt. The Syrian Uprising had begun.

March, 24th: Shaykh Said Ramadan al-Bouti's Lesson

On the evening of Thursday March 24th, Shaykh Muhammad Said Ramadan al-Bouti[4] made his way to Damascus' al-Iman Mosque in the Mazra' neighbourhood to deliver his weekly lesson. The main hall of the mosque was filled near capacity. Bouti's lessons are broadcast live on satellite television and are uploaded on his website, and thus have an audience greater than the few hundred in the mosque. That evening, Bouti broke from his scheduled lesson in order to address what had come to fill people's minds increasingly over the past week, saying, "Perhaps it is good, if I daresay not a duty, to say something concerning this strife (*fitna*) that has reared its head towards us."[5]

Bouti (b. 1929), an emeritus professor and former dean of the faculty of theology at Damascus University's Shari'a College, is Syria's most prominent religious scholar. A longstanding personal relationship developed between Bouti and Hafez al-Assad in the 1970s when Assad read one of Bouti's books, *Naqḍ awhām al-mādiya al-jadaliya* (Critique of the Delusions of Dialectical Materialism). This led to a series of intermittent private meetings between the two men over the following decades. In the 1980s, after the Assad regime violently put down the uprising in Hama, religious practice in the public sphere came under harsh repression and membership in the Muslim Brotherhood became a crime punishable by death. Bouti was able to use his relationship with Assad to secure the release of thousands of prisoners in addition to opening of the public sphere to religion again in the 1990s. During this period, Bouti's ties to the regime became stronger despite the fact that Bouti has never held an official position in the state religious apparatus. Bouti's rank as a senior scholar and his influence with the government has led to a pragmatic relationship between Bouti and the Assad regime. This relationship however is seen by many of his critics, including those amongst the 'ulama, as reflecting Bouti's political naïveté and his co-optation by the state.[6]

That evening, his speech covered four points, which would foreshadow part of the government's narrative concerning the protests. The first dealt with what was ostensibly the reason why protests took place throughout the Middle East, namely, the question of reform (*iṣlāḥ*). Reform here referred to changing those laws that block people's freedoms, as well as the corruption that results from such repressive laws. Bouti maintained that reform was a social and religious obligation, but posed the question: by what means is reform to be achieved? For Bouti, reform required two sides, those in power and those taking to the streets. He argued that the path of reform consisted in these two sides meeting (*talaqqī*), consulting (*tashāwur*), negotiating (*mudhākara*), cooperating (*ta'āwun*), coming to agreements (*ittifāq*) and then setting out to execute those reforms (*intilāq*) on a timeline. Reform, he emphasized, cannot be one-sided and cannot be realized by a faction of people that take over some square or street, carrying banners and chanting slogans. "A revolution," he said, "can destroy in hours, whereas building does not come to completion except in stages – [namely], those mentioned previously."[7]

The second point that Bouti addressed was the new reform program that had ostensibly already begun in Syria, a program that he claimed entailed fundamental reform (*al-islāḥ al-jadhrī*) and that was a result of the steps just outlined. He was referring to a venture initiated by Syrian president Bashar al-Assad, wherein the latter called a meeting (Bouti did not mention when this took place) with a number of 'ulama and Syrian intellectuals in order to hear the needs of the country and the shortcomings that those in positions of office needed to address. According to Bouti, in that meeting, "everything that might occur to the minds of those that are raising banners was laid out and discussed,"[8] followed by pledges to see the proposed suggestions realized. He stated that in the immediate future, announcements of fundamental reform (*al-islāḥ al-jadhrī*) that the nation had been awaiting and was in desperate need of were going to be made.

The third point concerned the origins of the protests in Daraa. Here, Bouti echoed what was the government narrative concerning the protests, namely that these protests did not truly reflect the concerns of the local citizenry and that they originated from outside Syria. He distinguished between the situation in Syria and what had occurred in Egypt, pointing out that the protests in Egypt had been organized locally, by individuals that were well known to the populace. The same, he argued, could not be said for Syria. Here he explained that the calls to protest were received from anonymous sources electronically, in a prepackaged manner, delineating what days to protest, what to call those days (Day of Anger, Day of Honour, etc.), the chants to use, what slogans to write on banners and so on. Bouti mentioned that he had himself received a number of anonymous pleas to use the Friday prayer as an opportunity to stage protests and that he tried to determine the source of these communiqués. The effort proved futile and this, according to Bouti, was reason enough to pause for consideration. The question that concerned Bouti was, given the anonymous and pre-packaged nature of these messages, how should one react in such a situation? For Bouti, the Qur'anic verse, "Pursue not that which you lack knowledge of," (Q. 17: 36) spoke to the current situation. The verse said to him,

> "Do not follow those who would take you by the hand to whence you do not know; do not follow someone you do not even know who they are; do not put your hand in the hand of someone you do not know; and do not put your hand in that of someone you know, but you do not know to what end they will take you."[9]

Given the unknown source of these calls, a number of possibilities seemed reasonable to him. Reflecting a culture where conspiracy theories of all sorts are given credence, he asked: was it not possible that Zionist Israeli hands were instigating matters? Is there not a likely possibility that those that "lie in wait" against Syria are behind this? Could it not be conceived that the American right-wing is behind these protests? Similarly, is it not a possibility that they are using the name of "reform" and "rights" to ignite the fire of civil strife in Syria? (The possibility that the protests were based on legitimate long-standing political, social and economic grievances of the population is conspicuously absent.) Thus, based on the intimations of this Qur'anic verse just cited and the unknown sources of these calls, discernment (*wa'i*) told him that it was not possible for him to blindly obey these calls.

He then described the situation of the previous Friday (March 18th), when a group of people had tried to start a protest after the prayer in the Umayyad Mosque. According to Bouti's account, the situation in the mosque after the prayer had ended was normal. However, outside of the mosque, according to Bouti, a group of people that had not been part of congregation lay in wait for the prayer to end and then had started shouting anti-government slogans. The congregation making its way out of the mosque sought to drown the protestors out by chanting religious invocations. Bouti's description of them–"their foreheads do not know prostration," "their bodies do not know how to bow," etc.– pointed towards their lack of concern for religion and the instrumental usage of the mosque as the communiqués had urged. This indicated to Bouti that these protests were ill intentioned, lacking any concern for religious teachings.[10]

For Bouti, the sum of all this, and this was the purpose of his intervention that night, was that such a method of reform (i.e. public protests) could only lead to violence and destruction and that the only way of attaining the desired reforms was through engaging the government through dialogue. The Sunni juristic principle that "preventing harm takes precedence over attaining benefits" (*dar' al-mafāsid muqaddam 'ala jalb al-maṣāliḥ*) needed to be applied. Given that the harm from protests–civil strife (*fitna*) and destruction–outweighed any potential good that might come from protests, Islamic reasoning could not mandate the protests.

The fourth point of his lesson that night was a heart-felt plea for people to turn to God in supplication during this period of trial to help see the nation through it. He repeated these four points in an interview for Syrian national television, which only convinced the opponents of the protesters. The next morning Bouti travelled to the Emirates and then to Brunei to participate in a conference for the following two weeks.

March 25th: Shaykh Usama al-Rifa'i's Sermon

The day after Bouti's lesson, on Friday March 25th, the slow-brewing tension felt throughout Syria boiled over into Damascus. The day before saw the most violent crackdown in Daraa since protests began and human rights groups reported over one hundred people killed.[11] That Friday, Shaykh Usama al-Rifa'i, one of Damascus' most influential 'ulama, made the demands of the protestors the subject of his sermon. Rifa'i is the eldest son of Shaykh 'Abd al-Karim al-Rifa'i (d. 1973), a Damascene scholar that set up a network of charitable organizations based at the Zayd Mosque in the Bab Srije neighbourhood. In addition to his outreach and charitable work, Shaykh 'Abd al-Karim was a prominent figure in the revival of religious knowledge in the middle of the last century.[12] His two sons, Usama and Sariya, had lived in exile in Saudi Arabia from the 1980s onwards, during which the charitable organizations of their father functionally ceased working. Upon their return in the mid-1990s these charitable networks were infused with new life and activity and came to be important religious institutions. Based in their father's former mosque and the 'Abd al-Karim al-Rifa'i Mosque (named after their father) in Kefer Souseh, the two brothers continue their father's method of outreach, focusing on charity and religious education. As Thomas Pierret and Kjetil Selvik[13] have illustrated, the "Zayd movement" (*Jamā'at Zayd*) has maintained an ambiguous relationship with the regime. On the one hand, their charitable work relieves poverty-related problems that the regime is unable to address, and for this reason is welcomed by the state. A sign of this approval is that president Assad met with Usama al-Rifaʻi and that the organization has received various state benefits (permission to raise funds, control of mosques, etc.). Yet, the movement has successfully maintained its independence and has resisted becoming a mouthpiece of the regime. They have been able to do this because of the movement's middle class merchant social base from which it derives financial independence. This point—remaining free of state money or interference—was emphasized by their father and is an important part of the movement's image. Their ideological independence is manifest in their sermons and lessons, in which they openly criticized elements of the state that they see as acting contrary to Islamic norms.[14] Rifaʻi's sermon that Friday reflected this independence.

After opening his sermon with a short discursus on security and the duty of preserving security, he said, "What we see in our country–what is going on from a week ago, more or less, and continuing until today–in Daraa and in other places, all of this obligates us to consider the duty of *naṣīḥa* that the prophet has commanded us to perform." *Naṣīḥa* is the notion of "sincere counsel" or "advice" and in Islamic discourse derives from the hadith, stating that religion consists of sincere counsel "to rulers of the Muslims as well as the common Muslim."[15] The act of *naṣīḥa* is a morally corrective form of criticism delivered when the advisor senses that a particular matter needs to be addressed. When directed to a sovereign by a religious scholar it is not an act of revolution or rebellion but rather an act of moral and "corrective" criticism. In his study of the *naṣīḥa* delivered by Saudi ʻulama to King Fahd during the Gulf War, anthropologist Talal Asad notes that their criticism did not offer a political alternative or attack the government but rather took the stance of a moral critic.[16] Criticism of the ruler in this form should not be conflated with civil disobedience and certainly not rebellion (*khurūj*), which in fact is disclaimed and deemed strife (*fitna*). Rifaʻi's sermon should thus not be seen as anti-regime or conflated with the Tunisian and Egyptian revolutions, which called for outright regime change—"the masses want to bring down the regime" (*al-shaʻb yurīd isqat al-nizam*). Rather, his sermon should be seen as a moral witness to the regime regarding the events in Daraa.

In his calm and reflective tone, Rifaʻi directed his sermon to "the president of the republic and to all those brothers in positions of responsibility (*al-masʼūliyūn*)" and then articulated the demands of the protestors. The key issue that everything rested upon was the notion of freedom. Freedom, Rifaʻi argued, is an essential component to one's humanity that distinguishes mankind from other creatures. To have one's freedoms taken away from them, completely or partially, is to lose part of one's humanity. He cited the saying of the second caliph 'Umar ibn al-Khaṭṭāb, rebuking one of his governors that mistreated a Coptic Christian, "Why have you enslaved people whose mothers gave birth to them as freemen?" The connection to Syria is clear: the population deprived of freedoms by the state has functionally been reduced to slavery and deprived of part of their humanity. The way in which Syrians have been deprived of their freedoms has been through the emergency laws implemented in 1963, which enshrined the authoritarian structure of the Baath government: "The emergency laws," Rifa'i said, "have curtailed all of the freedoms that should be enjoyed by any non-colonized nation." To restore these fundamental human freedoms and the humanity of the protestors, the emergency laws had to be repealed. Rifa'i provided an example of how the emergency laws suppress freedom by mentioning the countless political prisoners and prisoners of conscience in Syrian jails whose crime amounted to little more than a thought-crime.

Rifa'i turned his focus to speak about matters relating to religion, given that he was speaking from a pulpit as a preacher, and left it to specialists of other fields to speak about those. As an example of where freedoms relating to religion were curtailed, he mentioned the increasing secularization of public spaces that intruded on personal freedoms. Rifa'i was referring specifically to the 2010 ban by the Ministry of Education on female teachers in public schools and female students at university wearing face-veils (niqāb). The ban resulted in over one-thousand teachers being dismissed from their jobs. The Minister of Education, 'Ali Sa'd, said in newspaper interviews that these decisions were meant to preserve secularism by fighting fundamentalism and that they would be followed up by more decisions of this kind. [17] The problem for Rifa'i was not secularism per se, which he understood as the state not adopting or promoting a particular religion; the problem was that the state was overstepping its bounds and obstructing personal freedoms, proscribing individual choice. Such acts, Rifa'i said, evoked memories of September 29, 1981 when the Daughters of the Revolution went through the streets of Damascus and tore off women's hijabs.

Related to this, the Ministry of Education had verbally given orders prohibiting any manifestation of religion in schools, in addition to prohibiting the promotion of any form of religious activity, such as reciting Qur'an on the bus to and from school, memorizing hadith, conducting prayers in school, etc. These decisions were particularly intrusive in that inspectors were sent to schools to ensure that they were in conformity. In addition to repressing religion, this re-enforced a culture of spies and informants that has kept Syrians in a state of perpetual suspicion and mistrust for decades. Such orders were given verbally, Rifaʻi claims, so that there would not be a paper trail and so that the Minister of Education could claim deniability.

Another example of the aggressive secularization pertained to the governor of Damascus, Bishr al-Sabban. Sabban purged the bureaucracy under him of dozens of employees because of their open religious practice. Further, Sabban changed ten of Damascus' neighbourhood parks (out of 120) from being women's-only to being inclusive of men as well. Rifaʻi remarked that after sitting in extended meetings with the governor and his representatives, the latter were unwilling to recognize requests for such segregated parks as legitimate rights of citizens i.e. of the residents of the neighbourhoods that asked for such parks in the first place. What compounded the frustration was the disrespectful, dismissive and harsh treatment they received from Sabban and his office. While the particular examples mentioned by Rifaʻi might not have been shared by his audience, they told a story that they were all too familiar with, namely, an intrusive and repressive state bureaucracy that curtailed individual and group liberties.

Lastly, Rifaʻi mentioned the corruption that pervades every level of the vast state bureaucracy and how repressive laws are only applied to the poor while the wealthy few are able to bribe their way out of any legal problems. He closed his sermon saying,

> "If our brothers that are in charge, and foremost amongst them the president, want to placate Daraa and places other than Daraa throughout the region, the key to placating them is in the hands of the president and all of those in charge. The key is in their hands! And it is to change all these things that I have just mentioned."

He closed the first half of his sermon by thanking President Assad for freeing a number of political prisoners as well as for increasing the salaries of government employees but did not fail to reiterate the above-mentioned points.

Immediately after the prayers, the congregation–in the hundreds– started chanting slogans of solidarity with the people of Daraa as well as what has become a popular slogan of the Syrian protesters, "God, Syria, freedom and nothing else" (*Allah, sūriyya, ḥurriyya, wa bass*). Security around mosques had been heightened since February and as soon as the protesting congregation came within range of security forces, the latter first locked the doors to the mosque to prevent the congregation in the mosque from joining the protest and then began beating the crowd outside with batons and tasers and rounding them up into buses. According to witnesses, Rifa'i made his way out of the mosque with a group of worshippers surrounding him and, when he came face-to-face with the security forces, he ordered them to stop the violence and to let the crowd protest peacefully. Witnesses state that the security forces ceased for a period until Rifa'i had left, at which point they renewed their crackdown.

A number of features from Rifa'i's sermon stand in contrast to Bouti's lesson. Rifa'i's sermon addressed not only the congregation present in his mosque but more importantly was directed towards the government, president Assad and those in positions of responsibility. By addressing the government, Rifa'i distanced himself from it but did not do so by adopting an oppositionist stance. Rather, Rifa'i's stance was that of a mediator between the government and the protestors. He was thus able to give voice to the protestors, articulating a number of their concerns while successfully managing to avoid establishing himself as an ideological leader of the protests. Further, his address to his congregation extended beyond those present to include inevitably those that would hear recordings of his sermons (which are regularly put online as well as distributed in bootleg copies) and he thus provided religious guidance pertaining to the protests. In addressing the government and the protestors, Rifa'i acted as a moral intermediary between the two, providing both sides with the requisite guidance to realizing security. Lastly, Rifa'i's stance vis-à-vis the protestors is one of qualified endorsement. Rifa'i said, in a statement that he has repeated many times that he supports protests so long as they are peaceful, demanding legal rights and the lifting of oppression. However, if the protests entail carrying weapons, killing, spilling blood, destroying public and private property (i.e. all of the things that constitute *fitna*) such protests are prohibited by Islamic teachings.

Bouti's lesson by contrast was aimed at the populace. This stance was not a mediating position like Rifa'i's, rather it placed him on the side of power, making a case by providing a series of reasons for why the general populace should not participate in the protests and in fact be suspicious of them. By re-assuring the populace that reforms were underway, Bouti rejected the possibility of protests achieving reforms because whatever one might hope to gain from protests was already ostensibly in the process of being realized. What is absent from Bouti's lesson was any sense of the demands of the protestors besides a vaguely conceived notion of reform. Where Rifa'i's sermon sought to have the government soften its heavy-handed crackdown and to give ear to the protestors, Bouti's lesson sought to reduce the protests by having the protestors give ear to the promise of reform. Both however did not take the government to task for its use of violence.

These differences notwithstanding, *naṣīḥa* as a means of engaging the government is not precluded as an option for Bouti or any figure that takes a stance with the government. In the case of Rifa'i, this *naṣīḥa* is very public, made on the pulpit in front of hundreds and distributed to wider publics through electronic media. *Naṣīḥa*, however, can also be carried out in private and in most situations this is favoured because it safeguards other aspects of Islamic ethical teaching, such as protecting people's reputation, saving them from slander, backbiting, tale-bearing, etc.[18] In the case of *naṣīḥa* to the state, delivering the *naṣīḥa* in private safeguards against riling up the populace and does not publicly question the authority of the state. Bouti, for his part, has shown that this is how he employs *naṣīḥa* and his ability to influence the regime in the past demonstrates the utility of this approach.

March 25th: Shaykh Yusuf al-Qaradawi's Sermon

That same Friday, Shaykh Yusuf al-Qaradawi delivered a sermon in Qatar that also focused on the uprising in Syria.[19] The Azhari trained scholar has a history of political agitation from his youth and had been arrested by King Farouq of Egypt and the regime of Gamal Abdel Nasser a number of times. He left Egypt in the 1960s to head the Qatari Secondary Institute of Religious Studies and has lived in Qatar since. As a prolific writer, many of his key books have been re-published by local presses in the Arab world, ensuring greater distribution and readership, and have even been translated into European and other Islamicate languages (Urdu, Malay, Turkish, etc.). When the al-Jazeera network was launched in 1996, the weekly show *al-Shari'a wa al-Hayat* (Shari'a and Life) became a stage for Qaradawi to reach a greater audience and convey his message of Islamic modernity. Through these means, as well as tireless lectures given throughout the world, Qaradawi is undoubtedly one of the foremost transnational 'ulama today. Additionally, he is perhaps the most prominent and vocal champion of the Arab Spring amongst the 'ulama. In the heat of the protests in Egypt, many protestors looked for support from Egyptian 'ulama that had become popular in the last decade amongst a new generation, in particular the Mufti of the Republic Shaykh Ali Gomaa and the Shaykh of al-Azhar Shaykh Ahmad al-Tayyib. Both scholars however, cautioned the populace against descending on Tahrir Square and in fact told the protestors to return home.[20] Qaradawi, by contrast, encouraged not only the youth but the entire country—Muslims, Copts, secularists, young, old, the entire spectrum—to descend on Tahrir Square. It is with little surprise that days after Mubarak's resignation it was Qaradawi that led the Friday prayers at Tahrir Square, crowning him, in a sense, the shaykh of the revolution.[21]

An important element of Qaradawi's thought dovetails with his transnationalism, namely his vision of pan-Islamism. The entirety of the Muslim *umma* thus falls under his sphere of concern. Reflecting this, three days after his sermon at Tahrir Square, Qaradawi pronounced a fatwa during an al-Jazeera interview, calling on the Libyan army to turn its guns away from the people and to turn them on Qaddafi. This pan-Islamic concern was also reflected in how Qaradawi conceived of Syria's status in the Arab Spring. For Qaradawi, there was an intrinsic bond between Syria and Egypt and for this reason he argued staunchly against the notion of Syrian exceptionalism. This notion had been articulated by various voices (including president Assad in a January 31st, 2011 interview with the *Wall Street Journal*[22]) to different ends but essentially maintained that Syria was somehow different from its neighbours and thus immune to the protests and the awakening that was sweeping the Arab world. While Syria clearly resisted the initial revolutionary surge in January and February 2011, the reactions throughout the country after the March crackdown in Daraa proved for Qaradawi the ineluctability of the revolutionary spirit and Syria's place in it. "Today the train of the revolution reached a station that it was bound to reach," he said, "it is the station of Syria."[23]

He spoke directly about the crackdown in Daraa and belittled the government's efforts to address the problem. The previous day, Bouthaina Shaaban, president Assad's political and media adviser, announced that "the Regional Supreme Council of the Arab Socialist Baath Party was considering lifting the emergency laws and considering implementing a law of political parties."[24] Qaradawi was dismissive not only of these "considerations" and the Regional Supreme Council, but the entire way of thinking.

> What is this body? Who gave them authority over Syria? The Baath Party has ended in the entire Arab world! All of these old political parties, their time has passed, their end has come. The Constitutional Party in Tunis, the National Party that is in authority in Egypt – these parties are finished. [...] What remains? The Baath Party [...] Who are you, Baath Party? [...] These people are backward. They live in a different time than we live in. We are in the age of the Arab revolutions! These people have not opened their eyes or ears! They do

not open their eyes to see, or their ears to hear. They do not open their heads and minds to think. They think with a different mind!²⁵

After dismissing the Assad regime's efforts to quell the uprising in Daraa, he turned his attention to Bouti, not mentioning his name explicitly but clearly intending him. He criticized Bouti on two accounts, what Qaradawi saw as Bouti setting himself up as a lawyer making the case for the government and Bouti's pejorative description of the protestors – "a mob," "foreign infiltrators," "their foreheads do not know prostration," etc. Qaradawi held the accomplishment of the Egyptian youth in the highest esteem and saw the Syrian youth as being essentially the same. To disparage the reputation of the Syrian protestors was to disparage the Egyptians and their revolution. Referring to Bouti's criticism of the Syrian protestors, Qaradawi said,

> "How unfortunate that the 'ulama have lowered themselves to this level! Rather than telling the tyrant to stop his oppression of people, to establish justice amongst the people, he praises him and insults those youth! The youth that established the Egyptian revolution, the youth of Tahrir Square!"²⁶

More brazen than this however was his swipe at the Assad regime's sectarian affiliation and the real power in the country. One sentence, said almost in passing, was to become the focus of much ire in Syria. Recounting a rare visit that he made to Syria during the Gaza War in 2008, Qaradawi described the relationship between the Syrian people and the Assad regime as follows: "I saw that the Syrian people treat him [i.e. Bashar al-Assad] as though he were a Sunni!" He expanded on this with an observation about Assad, namely that, despite being an intelligent, cultured and capable young man, he was "the prisoner of a cadre, the prisoner of a group that he cannot free himself of," and as a result saw everything through their prism. This is no doubt an allusion to the power structure that Bashar al-Assad inherited from his father's tenure as president, namely the army, the Baath party and the infrastructure of secret police. Qaradawi thus hits at the minority religious affiliation of Assad as well as the political arrangement of power at the top of the Syrian regime. For these reasons, Qaradawi was convinced that the problems could not be solved at their source.²⁷ However, his call for the Syrian people from all of its religious and ethnic groups to rise against the Assad regime fell on deaf ears. The sectarian swipes and calls for solidarity were all understood as sowing *fitna*.

Mufti of the Republic, Shaykh Ahmad al-Hassoun and The Regime's Narrative

In Bouti's absence, the Mufti of the Republic, Shaykh Badr al-Din Ahmad Hassoun (b. 1949), stepped up his own media appearances to get across the narrative of the government. Hassoun was formerly the mufti of Aleppo and succeeded Shaykh Ahmad Kuftaro (d. 2005) to the position of mufti of the republic upon the latter's death. A cadre of prominent senior 'ulama (including Bouti, Wahbe Zuhayli, Mustafa al-Khinn, Mustafa al-Bugha, etc.) were stepped over to appoint a more junior figure. One explanation circulated regarding his appointment is that the senior 'ulama were offered the position but had each declined. His short tenure as mufti has not been without controversy, as we shall see. Contrary to Kuftaro, who functioned as a spiritual leader of thousands of Syrians and was quietist and accommodationist in his engagement with the government, Hassoun functions more like a politician and spokesperson for the government than a mufti.

Hassoun began his March 26th al-Jazeera interview by saying,

> "We in Syria, dearly beloveds, rejoice in a joy that cannot be exceeded because we have attained–as a people and as leaders–that which our brothers in Tunis and Egypt and the rest of the Arab world have attained, without their being anguish and spilling of blood, [contrary to what] many brothers have claimed and as many noble scholars have called people to [spilling of blood] yesterday in their Friday sermons throughout the Arab world."[28]

He referred to such people, with Qaradawi clearly in mind, as "sermonizers of *fitna*," that want "the Syrian people to be torn apart with sectarianism."[29] When asked about the reported deaths of dozens of protestors, Hassoun promised swift justice against the excesses of those involved in the Daraa crackdown but stayed on point about the foreign source of the protests. Throughout the interview, images from cell phones showing the crackdown of protests spoke louder and clearer than Hassoun's narrative.

That week, Hassoun made a trip to Daraa and visited the 'Umari mosque, which had become the centre of the protests and thus the scene of the most violent crackdowns. After seeing matters with his own eyes, he seems to have been deeply moved, as is testified to by the recording of a speech that he gave there and as some of my contacts close to the mufti informed me. Thereafter he maintained a low profile, working behind the scenes to calm the masses and appeared on Syrian television only occasionally, staying on point with the government's narrative.[30]

The government's narrative against the protestors was in full swing by this time. Syrian television had replaced its regular programming with almost round the clock coverage of events from the government's Syrian Arab News Agency (SANA). Their narrative of the events was that the source of the protests was not Syrian in origin, but was instigated by foreign infiltrators (*mundassīn*)—Israel, America or someone else—preying on the naïveté of teenagers. Syria, the argument continued, was unique in the Middle East because of its stability, its security and the absence of sectarian fighting. This foreign hand, so the logic of the narrative went, was seeking to disrupt these achievements through protests and civil strife because of Syria's oppositionist stance in world politics (i.e. anti-Israeli and anti-American expansionism). In other versions of this narrative, the protestors were being instigated by the Assad regime's bogeyman, the Muslim Brotherhood and Salafi-cum-Jihadi activists or the global bogeyman, al-Qaeda. Regardless of who exactly was the source of troubles in Syria, this looming threat necessitated the emergency laws, whose fruit was the relative stability and security that existed in Syria.

April 1: More Protests in Damascus, Shaykh Kuraym Rajih's Sermon

The following week, on Friday April 1st, protests occurred in Damascus again, this time in two locations: again at the Rifa'i Mosque in Kafar Souseh after Rifa'i's sermon and, this time also, in the Midan neighbourhood after Shaykh Kuraym Rajih's sermon at the al-Hasan Mosque. Rajih (b. 1926) is an internationally recognized authority in Quranic recitation, which has a strong popular base in Midan. He is also an heir to the efforts of Shaykh Hasan Habannaka (d. 1978), who, along with Shaykh 'Abd al-Karim al-Rifa'i, was instrumental in reviving Islamic practice in Damascus during the middle of the last century. Habannaka, in addition to being the teacher of a generation of Damascus' most pre-eminent scholars (including Bouti), is also noted for his opposition to the political moves made by the Baath Party in the 1960s and 70s that consolidated its control of the state. In 1965, for example, Habannaka led a march of 20,000 people through the city as a response to an anti-religious article published by an army magazine. When Habannaka was arrested, the souqs of Damascus closed in protest, demanding his release.[31] Rajih was Habannaka's most valued student and had accompanied his teacher in these various incidents.

Rajih's sermon, like Rifa'i's, did not actively promote protests; rather, he framed his sermon in a call for people to turn to God and for there to be a greater place for religious practice in people's lives. He then spoke at length about freedom and the demands of the people. In doing so, he targeted two elements of the government's narrative vis-à-vis the protests. The first was the government's claim that emergency laws guaranteed the security that all Syrians enjoy; he said, "We want to live, we want freedom, we want dignity – [we want] that people feel that they can sleep at night without any fear in their heart that they might be called in [the next morning], to go there, to go here, etc. The emergency laws are a problem; if they go and are replaced with laws against terrorism, this is worse!"[32] (This was what the government was considering and eventually did enact)

More importantly, he targeted the claim that these demands were a result of instigators from outside:

> I hope that this sermon which I delivered with the intention of a brief word, from the mouth of a man giving sincere counsel (*nāṣiḥ*), from the mouth of a man that has jealous concern for Syria, jealous concern for the Arab world, jealous concern for the Islamic world. Right now, I do not hold a position, nor do I run a centre [of learning], nor do I demand a greater salary than what I have; I am on the edge of my grave, so understand that with these words I intend an exhortation. It is fitting for a person after reaching 90 years of age to address the ruler of the land, to address the leader of the people, to address the army and to address the secret police. A man that has reached this age, who has lived close to a century of time, with everything that has happened to him, he has the right to say these words. Indeed, so take my words as those coming from a sincere counsellor. I am a Syrian man, I live in Syria, my father is in Syria, my grandfather is in Syria, my great grandfather is in Syria, my children are in Syria, my family is in Syria, I desire of Syria that Syria be the leader of the world. Syria, *Syria*! That Islam lead the world, that *la ilaha illa Allah* (there is no deity except for God) lead the world. [...] This is what I want.[33]

By emphasizing his age, his words invoked in the audience the respect due to an elderly and revered scholar; coupled with his emphasis of his autochthonous lineage it allowed him to take a nationalist stance justifying demands that could be claimed by the government to threaten the sense of national unity. In this rhetorically powerful manner he refuted the claim of foreign infiltration and grounded the demands of the protestors in the Syrian people. After addressing the government, he turned his address to the attendees demanding of them not to confuse matters (i.e. not to participate in protests), warned against using the mosques for other than devotions and threatened to not give sermons anymore should they protest from his mosque. Despite his request, that afternoon, a group of over 200 people made their way from the mosque to a local police headquarters. This protest was eventually broken up.

Bouti's Return

Bouti returned from his overseas travels to deliver his April 4th lesson at the al-Iman Mosque and used it to address the escalating events in Daraa.[34] His tone was sombre as he expressed his condolences to the families that had lost relatives in the crackdowns. He re-iterated the argument that he had laid out before his travels, namely that the only path to true reform was that of dialogue between the state and representatives from civil society. A revolution, he re-iterated, and the protests that precede one, are one-sided attempts at reform that will require the nation to pay a price that will far outweigh the benefit that might conceivably be achieved through a revolution. The point of his talk that evening was that real reform was attained through dialogue and he wanted to illustrate that point with a real example. He informed his audience that, *before* the protests, he had sat with president Assad and mentioned the need to open the door to freedoms and that the time of single-party rule was over. According to Bouti, Assad had agreed to these suggestions and stated that he was going to take steps towards realizing these goals. The president had initiated a series of meetings with prominent figures in Syria's civil society wherein the path to reform was laid out. As evidence of the success of these dialogues, Bouti announced the following reforms that the Assad regime had promised pertaining to religion:

- All women that lost their jobs as teachers in the previous year for wearing the *niqāb* would be allowed to return.
- The establishment of a national institute for Arabic and Islamic studies with campuses throughout the country, whose degrees will be recognized by the government.
- The establishment of an Islamic satellite channel based in Syria that teaches "true Islam."

As for political reforms—specifically the lifting of Syria's emergency law, eliminating single-party rule and changing laws that limited freedoms—Bouti mentioned that the president has already enacted changes and that all that remained was to announce them, which would happen in the immediate future. Bouti closed the first half of his talk by asking rhetorically, "So let me ask you now, did dialogue benefit or not?"[35]

The second half of his talk focused on Qaradawi's sermon from ten days before. Bouti and Qaradawi have a history of disagreement, an important aspect of which pertains to relations to their respective governments, so it surprised no one that Qaradawi would make reference to Bouti in the same way that it surprised no one that there would be a response. Bouti expressed surprise at Qaradawi's encouragement of protests, what Bouti called a "mob method" of reform. He wondered at how a scholar of Qaradawi's calibre could prescribe a destructive method instead of a constructive one embodied in dialogue. He further expressed wonder that Qaradawi had not employed *naṣīḥa* when he had visited Syria in 2008 and had an audience with president Assad. Rather than singing praises of Syria as a resistance state and its continued opposition to Israel and America, he should have spoken frankly while in the president's presence instead of from a pulpit in Qatar. Bouti pleaded with Qaradawi to not let sectarianism cloud his thinking and to let religion arbitrate.

Lastly, Bouti closed the evening by praying *ṣalāt al-ghā'ib*, a funeral prayer for those who have died in a distant place. This sent a mixed message. On the one hand, to pray *ṣalāt al-ghā'ib* for the dead in Daraa and Douma was to treat them in some form or another as martyrs. To suggest that they were martyrs further entailed that they were killed unjustly, which was suggestive of the government's culpability. Thus, rather than deflecting from the government's excesses and heavy handedness, the prayer in fact brought the question of the moral status of the government and the protestors to the fore, valorizing the latter and blaming the former.

The exchange between Qaradawi and Bouti is particularly significant because it figures prominently and exemplifies the war of narratives surrounding the Syrian protests. As noted above, Qaradawi made indirect reference to Bouti and the Syrian 'ulama that stood by the regime to which Bouti and Hassoun responded, directly and indirectly respectively. The regime maintains that foreign agents are the cause of problems and can point to figures such as Qaradawi as examples of irresponsible foreign sermonizers sowing discord and sectarianism in Syria. Bouti's dispute with Qaradawi however is different in nature than that between Qaradawi and the regime. Qaradawi, as noted earlier, is a pan-Islamic transnational scholar and is therefore not bound to a nation. He can thus maintain ideals of Islamic governance and adopt a confrontational stance because he is a scholar in exile.[36] Bouti, however, is a scholar bound to a nation. When the majority of Syria's most prominent scholars fled in the late 1970s and 80s, Bouti and a few others stayed behind and fought to keep Islam in the public sphere. Despite having a transnational influence (though substantially less extensive than Qaradawi's), Bouti's particular concerns are tied to the interests of the Syrian nation but not necessarily the Syrian state. In his own way, he distances himself from the regime and uses his influence to ensure that the goods of religion are realized, but he does so with a concern for Syrian society in mind. His pragmatic approach to engaging the Assad regime therefore requires a far more diplomatic posture than that of Qaradawi. The national concerns thus impose a constraint on Bouti's discourse that Qaradawi does not have.

April 8th: Shaykh Muhammad al-Yaqoubi's Sermon

In early April, Maher al-Assad, the president's younger brother and head of the army's Fourth Division and the Republican Guard, was dispatched to Daraa to deal with the protests. His forces led a systematic and brutal crackdown. Images and reports of the violence spread quickly throughout the country and evoked memories of the Hama Massacre in 1982. The parallels were not lost on anyone: Rifat al-Assad, who oversaw the month long crackdown in 1982, is the younger brother of then-president Hafez al-Assad. Outrage at the escalation of violence was widespread. Shaykh Muhammad Abu al-Huda al-Yaqoubi (b. 1963), who used to give sermons in the al-Hasan Mosque in the heart of Damascus, was one of the few Damascene 'ulama to express this outrage and demand that the violence cease. Yaqoubi is a descendant of the Prophet (*sayyid*) and comes from a family of 'ulama. He studied at the graduate level in Sweden and has a large international following as a result of years of teaching in North America and Europe. Upon returning to Damascus in 2006, Yaqoubi taught at various mosques, including the Umayyad Mosque, the mosque-shrine of the Sufi Muhyiddin ibn al-'Arabi and most recently the al-Hasan Mosque in the Abu Rumaneh neighbourhood in the heart of Damascus.

Yaqoubi directed his sermon in the al-Hasan Mosque on April 8th to the state administration. "Dear brothers," he said,

> "our land is being afflicted with strife (*fitna*) such that those near and far are speaking about what they see and hear, namely strife, affliction, killing and harm. We must provide an answer and advice (*nuṣḥ*) to the big and the small, the ruler and the ruled, the leader and the lead. The best advice is that which comes from the heart of a lover, one jealous of the religion of God, a lover of the country, jealously concerned that

it might be torn apart, jealously concerned about the blood of Muslims that it be shed unjustly."[37]

Yaqoubi explained the origin of the protests as follows:

> "We had hoped that path to reform would be hurried, because people are led by their aspirations. People were led to the streets [in protest] by long years of state oppression, when all they want is a bite to live on and freedom of expression. Between this and that, however, they took to the streets and we saw that our own people were being killed one after another in Daraa and in Douma, as though there were no dignity to human life."[38]

Yaqoubi proceeded to recite a litany of Quranic verses and hadiths about the nobility of God's creating man, the prohibition against oppression and the killing of innocents and the freedoms that God has made intrinsic to humanity. These textual citations were interspersed with commentary relating to the state of affairs in Syria pertaining to freedom of speech, to the information revolution that belied the state's narratives as well as to the equality between Muslims and non-Muslims in Islamic teachings in matters of justice. He advised the protestors and those witnessing them to stay within the bounds of Islamic teachings; that is, to keep the protests peaceful. The sermon was bold because many of the textual sources that he cited judged violence, oppression, the killing of innocents and tyranny as being tantamount to disbelief. While Yaqoubi never stated this conclusion explicitly, his sermon was meant to serve as a warning to the state of its grave moral position.

This sermon was uploaded to YouTube and created a buzz amongst Damascene and overseas watchers. Because of his April 8th sermon, Yaqoubi's mosque drew a substantial crowd the following week. Attendees from outside of the Abu Rumaneh neighbourhood came to al-Hasan Mosque, expecting to become an epicentre for protests in Damascus. The secret police had expected the same and were out in great numbers. Yaqoubi however diffused the situation, giving a five-minute sermon, stating:

> Many new faces have come to this mosque from various parts of the city. Some are expecting that there are going to be protests here and some have come to put an end to those protests, should they start. Let me state clearly, that I delivered a message last week that was my duty as an imam to give. The people of this neighbourhood are pleased with the leadership of Bashar al-Assad and are not interested in causing sedition and trouble. We welcome his efforts of reform and support him in that. If you came here for other purposes, please return back to

your own neighbourhoods and do what you want over there. We thank the president for his listening to the people and hope in his promise to implement reforms.[39]

This move by Yaqoubi should not be seen as a retraction of his previous position. Rather, it is consistent with the form of Sunnism shared by Yaqoubi, Rifa'i and Rajih, namely that provoking state-violence would be a greater harm than failing to hold the state morally accountable.

The Question of Sectarianism: Shaykh Moaz al-Khatib's Eulogies

The 'ulama thus far considered—Bouti, Hassoun, Rifa'i, Rajih and Yaqoubi—avoid the question of sectarianism almost completely, only addressing it as a danger to be cautioned against. This fear has promoted a culture that seems convinced that, if the Assad regime falls, Syria's heterogeneous religious and ethnic population—Sunnis, Alawis, Druze, Christians and Kurds—will turn against one another. The Assad regime, according to this logic, holds their mutual hostility at bay and in exchange for loss of certain freedoms it guarantees a certain amount of safety and security. For an older generation of Syrians, the civil war in Lebanon in the 1970s and 80s made the case for the previous Assad regime, while the sectarian fighting that has torn apart Iraq in the past decade looms large in the minds of many Syrians today. In such a milieu, Qaradawi's passing mention of the 'Alawi religion of the Assad's is construed as instigating civil war.

Shaykh Moaz al-Khatib (d. 1960) is one of the few 'ulama that has tackled the issue of sectarianism head on. As Maher al-Assad's forces cracked down in Daraa, Douma, a town on the northern outskirts of Damascus, erupted as another centre for anti-government protests that were also put down violently. Khatib is a scion from a family of 'ulama and is a geographer by training that worked for a petrochemical company for six years. He is the current president of *Jam'iyat al-tamaddun al-islami*, a reformist society formed in the late 1930s that published an influential journal.[40] He delivered a series of impassioned speeches at the funeral receptions in Douma, touching on a variety of issues. In one eulogy on April 6th, he addressed the fear of sectarianism in the following manner:

> We, in Syria, dear brothers–and this is not a blessing from the government but rather a blessing from God–we have lived all our lives as Muslims – Sunni, Shia, Alawi and Druze – with one heart;

alongside us, our noble brothers, those guided by the teachings of Jesus. [We have lived] with love, brotherhood and affection. The heart of one of us is not closed to his brother – he opens his heart, house and home to him. This is what we must persist in at all times. Our emotions should never make us leave this noble principle that we live by and that, God willing, we will die by.[41]

In the same eulogy, Khatib aptly expressed the feeling of the protesters vis-à-vis the discourse of fear:

"We do not look at anyone in this country in our emotions or in our hearts, with any kind of dislike or hatred. God forbid! We do this not out of fear of the government, nor from the secret police. The age of fear has ended. This is your country and you must save it" (ibid).

The previous day, Khatib had delivered another eulogy that sought to further refute the fear of sectarianism. In it, he went on the offensive against the regime by highlighting how particular Alawi tribes have been favoured at the expense of others.

It is no sin, dear brothers, for someone to be Sunni, Shia, Alawi, Druze, Ismaili or to be Arab, or Kurdish The value of a person to God is based on their piety. We are all one body. I say to you that the Alawis are closer to me than many people. I know their villages and the misery and injustice that they live with. We speak with freedom for the sake of every person in this country, for every Sunni, Alawi, Isma'ili, Christian, the Arab people or the great Kurdish people.[42]

The result of these speeches was that Khatib was called in for questioning by the security police on May 5th and was not heard from for over a month. He has remained silent since his release.

Protests Spread to the Outskirts of Damascus

Many of the large families in Douma had relatives living in other villages and towns surrounding Damascus, such as Saqba and Kafar Batna, and protests spread to these villages as well. With matters slowly nearing the city, stories of firsthand accounts of protests and government violence gained more circulation in Damascus. One such story that spread extensively in the circles of Damascene 'ulama was that of Mu'tazz-billah al-Sha'ar, a twenty-two year old law student at the University of Damascus whose family had links to the ulama. He was killed on April 22nd at a protest in his native Daraya. His story is illustrative of why many Syrian youth took to the streets. Sha'ar had attended Friday prayers at the mosques of Rifa'i and Rajih the previous weeks and had seen the government's violence against unarmed protestors firsthand. According to his father, witnessing these acts of violence politicized his otherwise apolitical son. On April 22nd, after Friday prayers at Rajih's mosque in Midan, the bulk of the congregation of a few hundred started chanting slogans of solidarity with the martyrs and made its way to a local police station. The young Sha'ar could not help but join. His father said that participating in the protest made him feel like he had lived for the first time in his life. Later that evening, returning to their home with his father and two brothers, security forces blocked the road into Daraya because a protest was taking place. Mu'tazz asked his father to join and as he made his way to the crowd, security forces opened fire. With nothing in his hand, chanting slogans of freedom, Mu'tazz stood his ground before the security forces and was shot twice in the chest. His father and brothers saw this from a distance and rushed to his body. The security forces prevented them from taking his body to a hospital and beat his father with batons as he repeatedly tried to take his son's dying body. Mu'tazz' two brothers, aged 15 and 17, were taken away and his father was finally able to take Mu'tazz' remains.[43]

This story spread quickly amongst many of Damascus' 'ulama because of the Sha'ar family's ties to various 'ulama. Given the familiarity of the people involved, this gave greater credence to this account as opposed to other stories filtering into Damascus about atrocities by the government. Yaqoubi referred to Sha'ar's story in another sermon on May 6th sermon, calling it "the story of one person, but it is in reality the story of dozens, and who knows, maybe hundreds of people."[44] He titled that week's sermon "The Illness and the Cure" and was unflinching in his criticism of the regime's failures, not only in the current crisis but also since the inception of the current regime. Yaqoubi emphasized that all of the problems that have led protestors to the street had their root "ten years ago," alluding to the failed Damascus Spring when democratic hopes were dashed by Bashar al-Assad's government. For Yaqoubi, matters had reached a point of no return because of the levels of violence.

> The problems of the past ten years could have been solved by the people and the government. [...] But the problem today between the government and the masses has reached a point of perhaps becoming unsolvable because it has reached the point of spilling innocent blood. Where can we get those innocent souls to give life to them again? A poor person can be made happy with an increase in livelihood, an

oppressed person can be made happy by freeing them; but how do you please someone whose son was killed? Someone killed by a sniper? Or a soldier killed by a civilian? Or an empty-handed protestor being killed? Or those who have been taken to hospitals wounded and then killed on the hospital bed? How can these be healed?[45]

Like Rifa'i and Rajih, Yaqoubi defended the rights of people to protest but emphasized that protests should not lead to *fitna*. He closed his sermon insisting (1) that the tanks and armed forces be called back from residential neighbourhoods and from around the townships, (2) that political prisoners and prisoners of conscience since the 1980s to the present be released and (3) that Syrians living in exile be allowed to return, mentioning the Muslim Brotherhood explicitly. At the end of this Friday prayer, he led a prayer for the martyrs that week. Unlike Bouti's performance of the prayer weeks before, Yaqoubi's prayer sent no mixed messages. The regime was the cause of people's grievances, was responsible for the violence and was unjustly killing its citizens who thus became martyrs.

As a result of this sermon, Yaqoubi was dismissed from his post on 12th May and was banned from public speaking. This was not an unfamiliar position for Yaqoubi. In the previous year, he had had a public dispute with Hassoun over comments that the latter had made that many felt were contraventions of Islamic teachings. Addressing a delegation from George Mason University's *Center for World Religions, Diplomacy and Conflict Resolution* in January 2010, Hassoun had said, "If our Prophet Muhammad asked of me to disbelieve in Judaism or Christianity, I would disbelieve in Muhammad," and also, "Had Muhammad commanded me to kill people I would have said to him that he was not a prophet." This meeting was reported in *al-Quds al-'Arabi* and was widely covered in the Arab and even Israeli media.[46] It was met with universal condemnation throughout the Middle East by 'ulama of virtually every orientation, including Qaradawi and Bouti. The most vocal critic of Hassoun on this issue however was Yaqoubi, who delivered a sermon in which he called for Hassoun to resign. In response, Yaqoubi was dismissed from giving sermons but was re-instated shortly thereafter but forbidden to teach. Thus, by being banned from delivering sermons, Yaqoubi was in familiar territory.

Yaqoubi left Damascus for Egypt, then the UK, and was active in opposition meetings in Istanbul by the National Salvation Congress. He has since based himself in Morocco. In September 2011, the al-Jazeera television show *Al-Shari'a wa al-ḥayāt* (Sharia and Life) had an episode on the Arab revolutions titled, "The Revolution: *Fitna* or Mercy?"

Qaradawi was present in the studio and Yaqoubi was interviewed briefly by phone where the latter made the case for not only the legality but the obligation of protesting against oppressive rulers (*al-imām al-jā'ir*).[47] Further, Yaqoubi explained that those 'ulama in Syria that remained silent vis-à-vis the Assad regime were to be excused because of the tremendous amount of pressure they are under. However, in regards to those figures that have spoken in defence of the government and authorized the latter's activities, Yaqoubi deemed them as being just as guilty as the government in tyranny and killing. The allusion to Hassoun was not lost on anyone. He closed by addressing the problem of the concept of *fitna*. Sunni thought has always held civil strife as anathema but Yaqoubi explained why this attitude did not apply in this situation:

> "The hadith and the words of the Prophet (upon him be peace and blessings) concerning civil strife (*fitna*), that is widespread, pertains to that [form of] strife wherein truth is not known from falsehood. As for this [case], truth and falsehood are clear now. Truth and falsehood are clear. Turning away from tyranny and disavowing tyrants, this is well known and understood. Likewise, supporting tyrants is forbidden, while helping the oppressed is obligatory."[48]

As events progressed in the uprising, Yaqoubi's stance as moral witness quickly gave way to moral condemnation of the continued and escalating violence. Though in exile, Yaqoubi's opposition to a state that he clearly deems illegitimate takes the form of providing discourses that authorize and, in fact, obligate protesting against the regime. Few of Damascus' 'ulama have taken such an oppositional stance against the government. The successes of the Arab Spring had emboldened some that have adopted this strategy, but for those like Yaqoubi, the regime's violence left them no other choice.

Developments over the Year 2011

The previous pages have documented developments amongst Damascus' 'ulama during the initial weeks in which the Syrian uprising began. Over the course of the year, many other 'ulama in Syria and outside have come to voice their opinions on the Uprising, virtually all of them condemning the government's violence.[49] During this time, the above considered positions taken by the various 'ulama have become more differentiated. The unrestrained violence against protestors has contributed to the hardening of the position of 'ulama like Rifa'i and Rajih. Their discourses have shifted from pressuring the regime to cease violence and enact reforms to total condemnation and demands for regime change. This shift, as the above narrative has documented, occurred much earlier for Yaqoubi.

The 'ulama that have remained in Syria, such as Rifa'i and Rajih, have been prohibited from speaking publicly at different times throughout the year while Khatib has been effectively silenced since release from his month-long incarceration in June. Perhaps the most telling sign of the regime's frustration with Rifa'i and Rajih occurred in Ramadan 2011. Violence continued throughout the sacred month and on the 27th night of Ramadan (August 27th, 2011)—one of the most sacred nights in the Islamic calendar—the Rifa'i Mosque was attacked by the government loyalist militia known as the Shabbiha. Rubber bullets were fired on the congregation, the mosque was ransacked and Rifa'i was wounded.

Bouti and Hassoun have become increasingly isolated and the target of harsher criticism by many inside Syria as well as sympathizers with the protestors outside. Hassoun has drawn even closer to the government after his 22-year-old son, Sariya, was killed in the town of Idlib on October 2nd. His son's killing has rhetorically been used by the regime to claim victimization and thus to justify its violence as a form of self-defence. Further, word of foreign powers potentially assisting the protestors in toppling the Assad regime (similar to NATO's role in Libya earlier in 2011) provoked the Mufti to say that Syria and Lebanon would send its sons and daughters to carry out suicide attacks on Europe and Palestine (i.e. Israel).[50] Bouti has come under harsh criticism from the Syrian public and also by other 'ulama for his continued denigration of the protestors and stubborn insistence on the government's account of events. In late June, he issued a fatwa on the impermissibility of protests that was met with scorn by the protestors.[51]

From the above narrative, I do not mean to suggest that 'ulama that are part of the state apparatus—whether officially like Hassoun or unofficially like Bouti—are unable to contest the state. Illustrative of this is the case of Shaykh Ibrahim al-Salqini, the mufti of Aleppo. As events were escalating in Tunisia and Egypt, Salqini had warned president Assad of the effects that the Arab Spring would have in Syria and told him to take pre-emptive action to avoid civil strife. In August, he and other 'ulama of Aleppo issued a declaration condemning the government's atrocities during the protests. Additionally, he had given a series of sermons condemning in strong terms the escalation over the summer. Salqini passed away on the 6th of September under conditions that many felt were suspicious, suggesting that the visits by the secret police during his final illness contributed to his demise. Despite being the mufti of Aleppo, Salqini contested the state's activities.[52]

By emphasizing the role of mosques and Friday sermons in the preceding pages, I do not mean to suggest that the protestors were all necessarily religious people. Despite the criticism that Bouti received, he accurately described the instrumentalization of the mosques. As protestors became more emboldened and widespread, mosques no longer served as the primary launching point for protests and other sites emerged alongside them, such as public squares and souqs. Further, the 'ulama seem to have lost (or perhaps never had) the ability to lead the protests or guide them, particularly after the emergence of the Free Syrian Army and other similar groups. The lack of reaction from the protestors to the attack on Rifa'i in Ramadan is suggestive of the 'ulama's inability to become symbols or even leaders of the protests. Finally, there are many more engagements between Syrian 'ulama and the regime that will need to be considered once the history of these events is written, particularly in the cities where the protests and crackdowns were at their largest.

Closing Thoughts

By way of conclusion, a few observations can be gleaned from the narrative provided above. Damascene 'ulama have taken a variety of stances vis-à-vis enacting change, shaped by the constraints imposed by the regime. Quietism is the predominant position adopted by Damascene 'ulama. As Yaqoubi explained, many have taken this position as a result of the intense pressure placed on them by the government. There are others still that are guided by Islamic teachings that label these events a *fitna*, wherein, according to tradition, 'the one sitting is better than the one standing', i.e. do not get involved.

The practice of *naṣīḥa* however counters quietism by imposing a moral obligation to, at minimum, not remain a silent observer. It presents a way of engaging the government as a moral critic, though (as discussed above), not placing one in confrontation with it. In the case of Rifa'i, Rajih and Yaqoubi, this *naṣīḥa* was done in a very public manner. The relationship of public *naṣīḥa* to protests is a complicated one. While *naṣīḥa* is not explicitly a call for protests, Rifa'i and Rajih's mosques had become centres for civil disobedience in Damascus. An unintended consequence of public *naṣīḥa* in an authoritarian regime, it seems, is that it feeds protests. Where freedom of expression has been suppressed for decades, voicing the opinions of the masses publicly turns into an unintended rallying cry. In this way, it feeds the opposition but remains detached from it; Rifa'i, Rajih and Yaqoubi did not march with the protestors or lead the protests.

This practice of *naṣīḥa* however can also be carried out in private, as Bouti mentioned in his lessons, noting that he had employed it. In this manner, it is consistent with a third option of engaging an authoritarian regime, namely to work pragmatically with the government. As we have seen, there is a difference in how this plays out as well. 'Ulama such as Hassoun act as part of the state, whereas Bouti has a more complex relationship. He stands apart from the official state apparatus but has an influence within it that he exploits towards securing goods pertaining to religion (banning of casinos, freedoms of religious expression, etc.). Working within the state apparatus thus does not preclude 'ulama from working towards change. As noted above, the mufti of Aleppo, Salqini, took active efforts to have the regime change its behaviour while holding office.

The constraints that the state places on the 'ulama cannot be emphasized enough. 'Ulama like Khatib have been thoroughly silenced because of these constraints, while Yaqoubi, not willing to accept such a fate, has been forced to leave Syria. 'Ulama in exile, such as Qaradawi and Yaqoubi, are able to be far more subversive and brazen in their attacks on the government. Other series of constraints however come into play, such as discursive ones relating to the particular Islamic traditions of learning the 'ulama in question adhere to.

It should be noted that these options–quietism, pragmatic engagement and moral witness and opposition–are not unique to the 'ulama. A decade before the Arab Spring reached Syria, the same options played out in the failed Damascus Spring, albeit not cloaked in the garb of religion.[53] On September 27th, 2000, ninety-nine prominent figures from Syrian society published a manifesto that came to be known as *The Statement of 99*. This statement addressed virtually the exact same issues as those of the Arab Spring (as Yaqoubi alluded to in his last sermon). It was prefaced with three paragraphs, a list of four demands (repealing the emergency laws, amnesty for political prisoners, implementing state laws guaranteeing freedoms and freeing public life from restrictive laws) and a concluding paragraph. The tone was conciliatory and hopeful throughout. The statement did not spark protests but an increase in civil society, with the proliferation of informal gatherings and discussions on the future of Syria's politics throughout the country. Two distinct approaches emerged as discussions ensued. One sought to engage the regime through a tacit alliance that would work toward gradual reform, consistent with *The Statement of 99*. The second took a confrontational stance towards the regime, based on the conviction that the regime was incapable of reform. In January 2001, a second statement was released, titled *The Statement of 1,000*, which reflected this second approach. This statement was prefaced by an essay that rehearsed how civil society was destroyed in Syria, implicating the regime of Hafez al-Assad throughout, and was strongly worded in its demands. The writing of this statement was contentious amongst the civil society activists and its release was not without controversy, given that a Lebanese newspaper leaked it before all the names associated with it signed it. The reaction of the regime was to turn the Damascus Spring into the Damascus Winter; the few steps towards liberalization taken by Bashar's government were pulled back and the most vocal opposition figures were imprisoned. The differences between the Damascus Spring and the Arab Spring are many, but the parallel that I am drawing attention to is how the 'ulama and the proponents of civil society sought to engage the regime in similar manners.

---

[1] An earlier version of this paper was presented at the University of St. Andrews' Centre for Syrian Studies 1st Postgraduate Conference, "Syria in a Changing World," September 1-2, 2011 and I thank Thomas Pierret for his response. I would also like to thank professor Malika Zeghal and Nuri Friedlander for comments on earlier drafts of this paper.

[2] For a broader picture of the various positions adopted by religious actors inside and outside Syria see Thomas Pierret's, "Syrie: l'Islam dans la révolution," *Politique étrangère*, 4 (2011): 879-891.

[3] Many of the sermons and public lessons that I analyze have been recorded and uploaded to social media websites such as YouTube and Facebook as well as websites maintained by followers of some of the 'ulama in question. By way of documentation I provide the web addresses to the relevant pages. All translations in this essay are the author's.

[4] For more on Bouti, see Andreas Christmann, "Islamic Scholar and Religious Leader: A Portrait of Muhammad Said Ramadan al-Buti." in *Islam and Modernity. Muslim Intellectuals Respond* (I. B. Tauris, London, 1998): 57-81. Also Jawad Anwar Qureshi, "Islamic Tradition in the Age of Revival and Reform: Said Ramadan al-Bouti and His Interlocutors" (PhD diss., University of Chicago, forthcoming).

[5] This lesson was placed online on a website that hosts recordings of Bouti's lessons, http://www.naseemalsham.com/ but has subsequently been edited to include only the last ten minutes of Bouti's speech. The author was present at this lesson and has his own recording upon which he relied.

[6] See Thomas Pierret, *Baas et Islam en Syrie* (Paris: Presses universitaires de France, 2011), 99-105.

[7] Personal recording.

[8] Ibid.

[9] Ibid.

[10] It should be mentioned that eyewitnesses whom the present writer has spoken with have disputed Bouti's recollection of events. Videos uploaded to

YouTube confirm their version of event. See for example http://www.youtube.com/watch?v=oD-YduvMM58 Last accessed April 20, 2012.

[11] For an account of this, see Human Rights Watch, *"We've Never Seen Such Horror" Crimes against Humanity by Syrian Security Forces* (New York: Human Rights Watch, 2011), 20-21.

[12] See Muhammad Muti' al-Hafiz and Nizar Abaza's *Tā'rīkh 'ulamā' Damishq fi al-qarn al-rābi''ashar al-hijri* (Damascus: Dar al-Fikr, 1986), 2:905-906.

[13] See their, "Limits of Authoritarian Upgrading in Syria: Private Welfare, Islamic Charities, and the Rise of the Zayd Movement," *IJMES*, 41 (2009): 595-614.

[14] Ibid.

[15] The entire hadith reads: The Prophet said, "Religion is sincere counsel (*naṣīḥa*)," three times, to which the Companions asked, "To whom, messenger of God?" He responded, "To God, His Messenger, the leaders of the Muslims, and their laity."

[16] See Asad's "The Limits of Religious Criticism in the Middle East: Notes on Islamic Public Argument," in his *Genealogies of Religion: Discipline and Reasons of Power in Christianity and Islam* (Baltimore, MD: Johns Hopkins University Press, 1993), 200-238. Compare with Malika Zeghal's study the *naṣīḥa* of the Moroccan Sufi Shaykh Abdessalam Yassine to King Hasan II in her *Islamism in Morocco: Religion, Authoritarianism, and Electoral Politics* (translated by George Holoch, Princeton: Markus Weiner Publications, 2008), 95-118. Yassine's *naṣīḥa* is more complex than that of Rifa'i or the Saudi 'ulama considered by Asad in that it functions as an admonition that de-sanctifies the Makhzan (Monarch) and is thus is more confrontational and subversive.

[17] *"Wazīr al-tarbiya yaṣdur qarār al-munaqqabāt min ḥaql al-ta'līm ḥifāẓan 'ala al-'almāniya,"* *France 24*, January 1, 2010, last accessed April 20, 2012, http://www.france24.com/ar/20100701-religious-laic-interdiction-niqab-syrie-education

[18] Cf. Asad's "The Limits of Religious Criticism," 223-227 for a discussion of *naṣīḥa* by Saudi 'ulama.

[19] For more on Qaradawi, see *Global Mufti: The Phenomenon of Yūsuf al-Qaraḍāwī* (edited by Bettina Grad and Jakob Skovgaard-Petersen London: Hurst & Co, 2009).

[20] Cf. Malika Zeghal, "What Were the Ulama Doing in Tahrir Square? Al-Azhar and the Narrative of Resistance to Oppression." *Sightings*, February 17, 2011. Last accessed April 20, 2012. http://divinity.uchicago.edu/martycenter/publications/sightings/archive_2011/02 17.shtml

[21] I use this phrase because he is the most prominent religious scholar to give unconditional support to the Arab Spring and based on conversations with activists in Egypt that have embraced Qaradawi because of this. The title of "shaykh of the revolutions" however has since been attributed to Shaykh Emad Effat. An Azhar graduate and senior official in Egypt's Dar al-Ifta', Effat attended every protest at Tahrir Square from the beginning of the revolution in

January. He was killed during a protest on December 16, 2011, by a gunshot to the chest.

[22] "Interview With Syrian President Bashar al-Assad," *Wall Street Journal*, January 31, 2011, last accessed April 20, 2012, http://online.wsj.com/article/SB10001424052748703833204576114712441122894.html

[23] http://www.youtube.com/watch?v=WJQnE9XuR4o Last accessed April 20, 2012.

[24] Ibid.

[25] Ibid.

[26] http://www.youtube.com/watch?v=ARhCWDjnI3o Last accessed April 20, 2012.

[27] http://www.youtube.com/watch?v=WJQnE9XuR4o Last accessed April 20, 2012.

[28] http://www.youtube.com/watch?v=8vqcuIOXEks Last accessed April 20, 2012.

[29] Ibid.

[30] http://www.youtube.com/watch?v=teQj_1aSRbg Last accessed April 20, 2012.

[31] See Patrick Seale, *Asad: The Struggle for the Middle East* (Berkeley: University of California Press, 1988), 115.

[32] http://www.youtube.com/watch?v=TmMhGC-rTYQ Last accessed April 20, 2012.

[33] http://www.youtube.com/watch?v=oito-uIOBOQ Last accessed April 20, 2012.

[34] For a transcript of this talk, see http://www.naseemalsham.com/ar/Pages/download.php?id=9716&fid=&file=../Component/word%20new/Arabic/Activities/syria.pdf

[35] Ibid., 7.

[36] It should be noted that in all of his talks about the Arab Spring, Qaradawi has been conspicuously less vocal about the protests in Bahrain, which suggests his concern for Qatar's geopolitical interests.

[37] http://www.youtube.com/watch?v=RTQHumyN5kM Last accessed April 20, 2012.

[38] Ibid.

[39] Personal recording.

[40] See Ahmad Mouaz al-Khatib, "Al-Tamaddun al-Islami: passé et présent d'une association réformiste damascène," *Maghreb Machrek* 198 (2009): 79-92.

[41] http://www.youtube.com/watch?v=nQJfz1DtSpk Last accessed April 20, 2012.

[42] http://www.youtube.com/watch?v=yAbBrpC8bWE Last accessed April 20, 2012.

[43] http://www.youtube.com/watch?v=1VM9o64sfbA Last accessed April 20, 2012.

[44] http://www.youtube.com/watch?v=o7Ozu1xDlgM Last accessed April 20, 2012.

[45] Ibid.

[46] Haaretz News Service, "Syria's Mufti: Islam Commans us to Protect Jusaism," *Haaretz*, January, 19, 2010, accessed February 5, 2012, http://www.haaretz.com/news/syria-s-mufti-islam-commands-us-to-protect-judaism-1.265712

[47] For a transcript of this program, see http://www.qaradawi.net/2010-02-01-08-43-29/5181.html

[48] Ibid.

[49] In this capacity, it is worth mentioning the Salafi Shaykh 'Adnan al-'Ar'ur, based in Riyadh, Saudi Arabia. Through his satellite show, he has called for armed revolt against the Alawite Assad regime. Closer to the positions of Rifa'i and Rajih is another Saudi based Syrian scholar, Shaykh Muhammad 'Ali al-Sabuni. Through YouTube and through al-Jazeera interviews, he has spoken out against the crackdown, accused Bouti and Hassoun of being "'ulama of the sultans" and hypocrites, and championed the rights of protestors.

[50] http://www.memritv.org/clip/en/3142.htm Last accessed April 20, 2012.

[51] All4Syria, "*Al-shaykh al-Būṭī: al-taẓāhur ḥarām...*," *All4Syria*, June 25, 2011, last accessed April 20, 2012, http://all4syria.info/web/archives/14878

[52] Roula Hajjar and Ellen Knickmeyer, "Syria: Death of Popular Sunni Cleric Stirs Unrest in Aleppo," *Los Angeles Times*, September 6, 2011, accessed February 5, 2012, http://latimesblogs.latimes.com/babylonbeyond/2011/09/syria-aleppo-sunni-cleric.html See also Thomas Pierret, "Le décès du Mufti d'Alep, coup dur pour l'opposition syrienne," *Le Blog de Thomas Pierret*, September 8, 2011, http://blogs.mediapart.fr/blog/thomas-pierret/080911/le-deces-du-mufti-dalep-coup-dur-pour-lopposition-syrienne.

[53] See Flynt Leverett's *Inheriting Syria: Bashar's Trial by Fire* (Washington, D.C.: The Brookings Institution, 2005), 91-94 and 203-212.

References

'Abd al-Satar, Muhammad, "Al-Tajdid fi al-Fikr al-Islami," lecture delivered on 7 March, 2009. Available at http: //www.syrianawkaf.org.
'Abd-Allah, U., F., *The Islamic struggle in Syria,* (Berkley: Mizan Press, 1983).
'Abd al-Satar, Muhammad, "Ai-'Alaqat al-Insaniya fi al-Islam" lecture delivered at the Asad Library, Damascus. Available at http: //www.Syrianawkkaf.org.
Asad, Talal, "The Limits of Religious Criticism in the Middle East: Notes on Islamic Public Argument," in: idem: *Genealogies of Religion: Discipline and Reasons of Power in Christianity and Islam* (Baltimore, MD: Johns Hopkins University Press, 1993), 200-238.
Ayoubi, N., *Political Islam: religion and politics in the Arab world,* (New York: Routledge 1991).
Batatu, Hanna, *Syria's peasantry, the descendants of its lesser rural notables, and their politics,* (Princeton: Princeton University Press, 1999).
Böttcher, Annabelle "Islamic Teaching among Sunni Women in Syria," in Bowen, Lee Domma, and Evelyn A. Early eds., *Everyday Life in the Muslim Middle East,* (Bloomington and Indianapolis: Indiana University Press, 2002).
_____, *Official Sunni and Shi'i Islam in Syria,* (San Domenic: European University Institute, 2002).
Al-Buti and Muhammad al-Habib al-Marzuki, *al-La Mazhabiya Akhtar Bid'a Tuhadid al-Shari'a al-Islamiya,* (Damascus: Dar al-Farabi, n.d.).
Al-Buti, Sa'id, *al-mazaheb al-tawhidiya wa al-falsafat al-mu'asira,* (Damascus: Dar al-Fikr, 2008).
_____, *al-Salafiya Marhala Zamaniya Mubaraka La Mazhab Islami,* (Damascus: Dar al-Fikr, 2006).
_____, *Kalimat fi Munasabat* (Words on Occasions), (Damascus: Dar al-Fikr, 2002).
_____, "Min al-Tataruf ila al-Hiwar" in *Mushkilat fi Tariq al-Nuhud,* (Damascus: Dar al-Fikr, 2001).
_____, *al-Ta'aruf 'ala al-Dhat Huwa al-Tariq ila al-Islam,* (Damascus: Dar al-Fikr, n.d.).
_____, lecture "Tawdhif al-Din fi al-Sira' al-Siyasi" [The employment of religion in the struggle for power], Damascus, March 2000.
Carré, O., and Michaud, G., *Les Frères Musulmans (1928-1982),* (Paris: Gallimard, 1983).

Christmann, Andreas, "'73 Proofs of Dilettantism: The Construction of Norm and Deviancy in the Responses to 'al-Kitab wa'l-Qur'an: Qira'a Mu'asira' by Mohamad Shahrour" *Die Welt des Islam* 45, 2005: 20-73.

_____, "Islamic Scholar and Religious Leader: A portrait of Shaykh Muhammad Sai´d Ramadan al-Buti," *Islam and Christian-Muslim Relations,* Vol. 9, No. 2, 1998.

_____, "Islamic Scholar and Religious Leader: A Portrait of Muhammad Said Ramadan al-Buti." in *Islam and Modernity. Muslim Intellectuals Respond,* London: I. B. Tauris, 1998: 57-81.

_____, "'The Form is Permanent, but the Content Moves': The Qur'anic Text and its Interpretation(s) in Mohamad Shahrour's *Al-Kitab wa l-Quran*," *Die Welt des Islam,* 43, 2003: 143-172.

_____, "Ascetic Passivity in Times of Extreme Activism: the Theme of Seclusion in a Biography by al-Buti," in Philip S. Alexander et al. eds., *Studia Semitica: the Journal of Semitic Studies Jubilee Volume,* (Oxford: Oxford University Press, 2005).

De Jong, Fred, "Les confréries mystiques musulmanes au Machreq arabe," in Alexandre Popovic and Gilles Veinstein (eds.), *Les Ordres mystiques dans l'Islam: Cheminements et situation actuelle* (Paris: Editions de l'EHESS, 1986).

Grad, Bettina and Jakob Skovgaard-Petersen, *Global Mufti: The Phenomenon of Yūsuf al-Qaraḍāwī* (London: Hurst & Co, 2009).

Habash, Muhammad, "al-I´tiraf bi al-Akhar Mas'ala Siyasiya Aydan," in Adeeb Khoury ed., *Ishkaliyat al-I´tiraf bi al-Akhar,* (Damascus, 2007).

al-Hafez, Muti´ and Nizar Abaza, *Tarikh Ulama Dimashq,* 3 Volumes, (Damascus: Dar al-Fikr, 1986, 1991).

Haji, Muhammad Umar, *'Alamiyat al-Da'wa ila allah ta'ala* (The Global Call to Allah), (Damascus: Dar al-Maktabi, 2007).

Hassoun, Ahmad Badr al-Din, "Suriya: Madrasat al-'Aysh al-Mushtarak," lecture delivered in Homs on 22 July 2009. Recording in Arabic available at: http://www.drhassoun.com/news/news_details.php?news_id=750.

_____, "Syria: an example for national unity," lecture delivered at the Arab Cultural Center, Damascus, on 28 June 2010.

Heck, L. Paul, "Muhammad al-Habach et le dialogue interreligieux," in Baudouin Dupret (ed.), *La Syrie au Présent,* (Paris: Sinbad / Actes Sud, 2007).

_____, "Religious Renewal in Syria: the Case of Muhammad al-Habash," *Islam and Christian-Muslim Relations,* 15, 2004: 185-207;

Hinnebusch, A. Raymond, *Syria: Revolution from Above,* (New York & London: Routledge, 2001).

Human Rights Watch, "We've Never Seen Such Horror" Crimes against Humanity by Syrian Security Forces (New York: Human Rights Watch, 2011).

Kalmbach, Hilary, "Social and Religious Change in Damascus: One Case of Female Religious Authority," *British Journal of Middle Eastern Studies,* 35, 2008.

Khatib, Line, Islamic Revivalism in Syria: The Rise and Fall of Ba´thist Secularism, (London and New York: Routledge, 2011).

al-Khatib, Ahmad Mouaz, "Al-Tamaddun al-Islami: passé et présent d'une association réformiste damascène," in : *Maghreb Machrek*, 198, 2009: 79-92.
Kuftaro, Salah, "Al-Wihda al-Islamiya wa Tahadiyat al-'Asr," *Nahj al-Islam*, 1 May 2009.
Kutchera, C., "Wither the Syrian Muslim Brothers", *Middle East Magazine*, April 1988.
Kutschera, C., "Syrie: l'éclipse des Frères Musulmans", *Cahiers de l'Orient*, No. 7, Volume 3, 1987.
Landis, Joshua and Joe Pace, "The Syrian Opposition," *The Washington Quarterly*, 30, 1, Winter 2006-2007.
Landis, Joshua, "The Syrian opposition : the struggle for unity and relevance, 2003-2008" in Fred H. Lawson (ed.), *Demistifying Syria* (London: Saqi Books, 2009).
Leif, Stenberg, "Young, Male and Sufi Muslim in the City of Damascus," in Jørgen Bæck Simonsen, ed., *Youth and Youth Culture in the Contemporary Middle East*, (Aarhus: Aarhus University Press, 2005).
_____, "Naqshbandiyya in Damascus: Strategies to Establish and Strengthen the Order in a Changing Society," in Elisabeth Özdalga, ed., *Naqshbandis in Western and Central Asia - Change and Continuity*, (Istanbul: Swedish Research Institute in Istanbul, 1999).
Leverett, Flynt, *Inheriting Syria: Bashar's Trial by Fire* (Washington, D.C.: The Brookings Institution, 2005).
Moubayed, Sami, "The Islamic Revival in Syria," *Mideast Monitor* 1, 3 (September-October 2006) available at http://www.mideastmonitor.org/issues/0609/0609_4.htm (Last viewed 3 May 2009)
Al-Nabusli, Muhammad Ratib, *Muqawimat al-Taklif*, (Damascus: Dar al-Maktabi, 2005).
Olson, W. Robert, *The B'ath and Syria*, (Princeton, N.J.: The Kingston Press, Inc., 1982).
Pargeter, A., The Muslim Brotherhood: the burden of tradition, (London: Saqi Books, 2010).
Perthes, Volker, *Syria under Bashar al-Asad: Modernization and the limits of Change*, (London and New York: Routledge, 2004).
Pierret, Thomas and Kjetil Selvik, "Limits of Authoritarian Upgrading in Syria: Private Welfare, Islamic Charities, and the Rise of the Zayd Movement," *International Journal of Middle Eastern Studies*, 41, 2009: 595-614.
Pierret, Thomas, "Syrie: l'Islam dans la revolution", *Politique Etrangère*. Vol. 4, 2011: 879-891.
_____, *Baas et Islam en Syrie* (Paris: Presses universitaires de France, 2011).
Pinto, Paulo, "Dangerous Liaisons: Sufism and the State in Syria," in Jakelic S. and J. Varsoke (eds.), *Crossing Boundaries: From Syria to Slovakia*, (Vienna: IWM Junior Visiting Fellows' Conferences, Vol. 14, 2003).
Qureshi, Jawad A., "Islamic Tradition in the Age of Revival and Reform: Said Ramadan al-Bouti and His Interlocutors" (PhD diss., University of Chicago, forthcoming).
Rabo, Annika, "Gender, State and Civil Society," Hann, Chris and Elizabeth Dunn, *Civil Society: Challenging Western Models*, (London & New York: Routledge, 1996).

Roy, Olivier, *The Failure of Political Islam*, (Cambridge: Harvard University Press, 1996).
_____, *Secularism Confronts Islam*, (New York: Columbia University Press, 2007).
Salem, Muhammad ʿAdnan, "Awaliyat al-Qiraʾa fi Hayat al-Insan, in *Mushkilat fi Tariq al-Nuhud*, (Damascus: Dar al-Fikr, 2001).
Salloukh, Bassel, "Organizing Politics in the Arab World: State-Society Relations and Foreign Policy Choices in Jordan and Syria," (McGill University: PhD Thesis, 2000).
Seale, Patrick, *Asad: The Struggle for the Middle East* (Berkeley: University of California Press, 1988).
Shahrur, Muhammad, *Tajfif Manabiʿal-Irhab*, (Damascus: al-Ahali, 2008).
Sibaʿi, Mustafa, *Asdaq al-Itijahat al-Fikriya fi al-sharq al-Arabi* [The Sincerest Intellectual Directions in the Arab East], (Damascus: Dar al-Waraq, 1998).
_____, *Islamuna* [Our Islam], (Damascus: Dar al-Waraq, 2001).
Torrey, G., "The Neo-Baʾath: ideology and practice", *Middle East Journal*, Vol. 23, No. 4, 1969.
US Embassy/Syria, "The Syrian Muslim Brotherhood", *US Embassy cable to State Department* (DAMASCUS 575, 26th February1985)
_____, "Khaddam's and Bayanouni's Faustian pact", *US Embassy in Damascus' cable to State Department* (C-NE6-00262, 18/4/2006)
_____, "Movement for Justice and Development seeking to expand role in Syria", *US Embassy in Damascus' cable to State Department* (DE RUEHDM 00185, 11/3/2011)
_____, "Murky alliances: Muslim Brotherhood, the Movement for Justice and Democracy and the Damascus Declaration", *US Embassy in Damascus' cable to State Department* (DE RUEHDN 000477, 8/7/2009)
Van Dam, Nikolas, *The Struggle for Power in Syria: Politics and Society under Asad and the Baʿth Party*, (London & New York: I.B. Tauris Publishers, 1996/ 2011^2).
Weisman, Itzchak, *Taste of Modernity: Sufism, Salafiyya, and Arabism in Late Ottoman Damascus*, (Leiden: Brill, 2000).
_____, "Saʿid Hawwa and Islamic Revivalism in Baʿthist Syria," *Middle Eastern Studies*, 29 October 1993:144-146.
_____, "The Politics of Popular Religion: Sufis, Salafis, and Muslim brothers in 20th-Century Hamah," *International Journal of Middle East Studies* 37, 2005: 37-58.
Wickham, Rossefsky Carrie, *Mobilizing Islam*, (New York: Columbia University Press, 2002).
Zeghal, Malika, "The *naṣīha* of the Moroccan Sufi Shaykh Abdessalam Yassine to King Hasan II," In: idem: *Islamism in Morocco: Religion, Authoritarianism, and Electoral Politics* (translated by George Holoch, Princeton: Markus Weiner Publications, 2008), 95-118.
Zisser, Eyal, *Commanding Syria: Bashar al-Asad and the First Years in Power*, (New York: I.B.Tauris, 2007).
_____, "Syria, the Baʿth Regime and the Islamic Movement: Stepping on a New Path?" *The Muslim World* Vol. 95, No. 1 (January 2005).

Interviews (R. Lefèvre)

Interview with Ali Sadreddine al-Bayanouni, London, 30/11/2011.
Interview with Obeida Nahas, London, 30/6/2011.
Interview with Malik el-Abdeh, London, 6/12/2011.
Interview with Zouheir Salem, London, 20/7//2011 and 2/10/2011.
Interview with Walid Safour, London, 22/9/2011.
Interview with Muhammed Hawari, Aachen, 19/11/2011.
Interview with Issam al-Attar, Aachen, 19/11/2011.
Interview with Abdel Halim Khaddam, Paris, 23/6/2011.
Interview with Burhan Ghalioun, Paris, 2/6/2011.
Interview with Muhammed Riyad al-Shuqfah, Istanbul, 9/9/2011.
The political perspective for Syria: the Muslim Brotherhood's vision of the future (London, December 2004, copy given to the author)
The National Charter of Syria (London, August 2002, copy given to the author)

Publications on the Web

Akhbar al-Sharq website at: www.thelevantnews.net
Cham Press at: www.champress.net
CIA World Factbook at: www.cia.gov/cia/publications/factbook/goes/sy.html
Elaph website at: www.elaph.com
Joshua Landis website, "Syria Rescinds Ban on Religious Lessons in Mosques" at: faculty-staff.ou.edu/L/Joshua.M.Landis-1/syriablog/index.html, 30 March 2006
Kuluna Shuraka' website at: all4syria.info/
Al-Marfa' website at: www.almarfaa.net/?p=243
Naseem al-Sham website at: http://www.naseemalsham.com/
Shaykh al-Bouti website at: www.bouti.com
Shaykh Ahmad Hassoun website at: www.drhassoun.com
Shaykh Khaznawi website at: www.khaznawi.de/khaznawi/2005/3.htm
Shaykh Kuftaro website at: www.kuftaro.org
Shaykh Qaradawi website at: www.qaradawi.net.
Shaykh Rajab website at: www.sheikhrajab.org
Shaykh Zuhayli website at: www.zuhayli.net
Syrian Awqaf website at: www.syrianawkkaf.org
Syrian Central Bureau of Statistics, 2009 Syrian Statistical Abstract at: wwwcbssyr.org
The Syrian Human Rights Committee at: www.shrc.org
Taghrib website at: www.Taghrib.org
Al-Tajdeed website at: altajdeed.org
University of Chicago, The Martin Marty Center: *Sightings* http://divinity.uchicago.edu/martycenter/publications/sightings/
Al-Zayd movement website at: www.sadazaid.com

Newspapers and News Channels

Arabiya TV.
Asharq Al-Awsat.
Bloomberg.
BBC World News.
The Daily Star.
Daily Telegraph.
Der Spiegel.
Foreign Policy.
France 24.
Guardian.
Gulf News.
Haaretz.
Al-Hayat.
Al-Jazeera TV.
Los Angeles Times.
The New York Times.
The New York Times.
As-Safir.
Syria Briefing.
Syria Times.
Teshreen.
Al-Thawra.
Wall Street Journal.
Washington Post.
Al-Watan.

About the Authors

Line Khatib is a senior research fellow at ICAMES (the Inter-University Consortium for Arab and Middle Eastern Studies), McGill University, and a visiting assistant professor at the American University of Sharjah where she teaches political science. She is the author of a number of works including *Islamic Revivalism in Syria: the Rise and Fall of Ba'thist Secularism* (Routledge, 2011). Her research interests lie within the fields of Comparative Politics, religion and politics, and authoritarianism and democratization in the Arab World, with a particular focus on Islamic groups as social and political movements.

Raphaël Lefèvre is a Gates Scholar and a PhD candidate at the University of Cambridge (King's College). He is the author of *Ashes of Hama: the troubled fate of Syria's Muslim Brotherhood* (Hurst, forthcoming 2012). His research interests are focused on the evolution of political Islam in the Middle East with a particular emphasis on Syria and Tunisia.

Jawad Anwar Qureshi is a PhD candidate in Islamic Studies in the University of Chicago's Divinity School. His dissertation studies developments in Damascus' religious field in the last century, focusing on Syria's most prominent religious scholar and is tentatively titled "Islamic Tradition in the Age of Revival and Reform: Said Ramadan al-Bouti and His Interlocutors." His research interests focus on Islamic thought in the modern age and its engagement with modernity.

The St Andrews Papers on Modern Syrian Studies is published by the Centre for Syrian Studies, University of St Andrews, Scotland and distributed by Lynne Rienner Publishers, Boulder, CO, USA. The series remit is to publish cutting edge contemporary research and analysis on modern Syria, with the focus on the contemporary economic "transition" (reform) and on Syria's current security problems.
http://www.st-andrews.ac.uk/~wwwir/syrian/

We invite submission of unsolicited papers, particularly papers that report on current empirical research on Syria. Send paper submissions to series editor, Raymond Hinnebusch, School of International Relations, University of St Andrews, St Andrews, Fife, Scotland, KY15 7SP, U.K. or by e-mail to rh10@st-andrews.ac.uk.

St Andrews Papers on Contemporary Syria

SERIES EDITOR, RAYMOND HINNEBUSCH

Agriculture and Reform in Syria
Raymond Hinnebusch, Atieh El Hindi,
Mounzer Khaddam, and Myriam Ababsa

Changing Regime Discourse and Reform in Syria
Aurora Sottimano and Kjetil Selvik

Civil Society and the State in Syria: The Outsourcing of Social Responsibility
Laura Ruiz de Elvira and Tina Zintl

State and Islam in Baathist Syria: Confrontation or Co-optation?
Line Khatib, Raphaël Lefèvre, and Jawad Qureshi

The State and the Political Economy of Reform in Syria
Raymond Hinnebusch and Soren Schmidt

Syria and the Euro-Mediterranean Relationship
Jörg Michael Dostal and Anja Zorob

Syrian Foreign Policy and the United States: From Bush to Obama
Raymond Hinnebusch, Marwan J. Kabalan,
Bassma Kodmani, and David Lesch

Syrian Foreign Trade and Economic Reform
Samer Abboud and Salam Said

Syria on the Path to Economic Reform
Samir Seifan

*Syria's Contrasting Neighbourhoods:
Gentrification and Informal Settlements Juxtaposed*
Balsam Ahmad and Yannick Sudermann

Syria's Economy and the Transition Paradigm
Samer Abboud and Ferdinand Arslanian